APPRECIATION FOR THE BOOK

I wrote a Facebook message to Gopi in mid-2016 in response to a short story he had written, which had really moved me. I remember writing: 'You're really talented, you should write a book.' I introduced him to my partner, Jim, who's also a writer and he described Gopi's writing as 'perfectly rendered'.

A little over a year later, we got an excited response back, and here's the book. Gopi is one of those rare people who can toggle between deep spirituality and deep pragmatism, and managed to bring both those to bear when we worked together at IDEO. I'm really happy that his book has come to fruition; the notion of bringing together mindfulness and creativity is the perfect topic to explore right now with the world around us in swirl and chaos. Gopi brings gravitas and centricity to the concept, while at the same time encouraging the reader to 'stay young, stay a beginner, stay playful'.

—**Paul Bennett**
Chief Creative Officer
IDEO

Gopi has created a wonderful guide to creativity and mindfulness. His playful writing style keeps you engaged, allowing the lessons to sink in. Reading this book will deepen your understanding of the role of creativity in our lives.

—**Haben Girma**
Disability rights lawyer, author and speaker
Forbes' 30 under 30 (2016)

Creativity Unleashed provokes us to think of the limitless potential of creativity in all of us. Gopi offers simple and doable exercises that would help one stay mindful and open-minded to innovative possibilities. An engaging read.

—**VR Ferose**
Senior Vice President and
Head of Globalization Services, SAP SE
Author and columnist

CREATIVITY UNLEASHED

CREATIVITY UNLEASHED

48 DAYS OF MINDFULNESS TO UNLOCK YOUR CREATIVE SPIRIT

GOPI KRISHNASWAMY

BLOOMSBURY
NEW DELHI • LONDON • OXFORD • NEW YORK • SYDNEY

BLOOMSBURY INDIA
Bloomsbury Publishing India Pvt. Ltd
Second Floor, LSC Building No. 4, DDA Complex, Pocket C – 6 & 7,
Vasant Kunj, New Delhi 110070

BLOOMSBURY, BLOOMSBURY INDIA and the Diana logo are trademarks of
Bloomsbury Publishing Plc

First published in India 2019
This export edition published in 2020

Copyright © Gopi Krishnaswamy 2019
Illustrations © Anamika Gopi 2019

Gopi Krishnaswamy has asserted his right under the Indian Copyright Act to be identified as
the Author of this work

All rights reserved. No part of this publication may be reproduced or transmitted in any
form or by any means, electronic or mechanical, including photocopying, recording, or
any information storage or retrieval system, without prior permission in writing from the
publishers

Bloomsbury Publishing Plc does not have any control over, or responsibility for, any
third-party websites referred to or in this book. All internet addresses given in this book
were correct at the time of going to press. The author and publisher regret any inconvenience
caused if addresses have changed or sites have ceased to exist, but can accept no responsibility
for any such changes

ISBN: TPB: 978-93-88038-706; eBook: 978-93-88038-71-3

Typeset in Manipal Digital

Bloomsbury Publishing Plc makes every effort to ensure that the papers used in the
manufacture of our books are natural, recyclable products made from wood grown in
well-managed forests. Our manufacturing processes conform to the environmental
regulations of the country of origin.

To find out more about our authors and books visit www.bloomsbury.com and sign up for
our newsletters

WHY 48 DAYS?

Because 48 is a special number in many traditions.

The duration of a mandala in the yogic system is 40 to 48 days. It is believed that any form of practice takes around 48 days to integrate into our system and produce results. It takes this much time to create space for the practice in our bodies and minds, and synchronise it with the environment.

Lord Buddha sat under a bodhi tree for 48 days until he attained enlightenment.

In Judaism, it is believed that wisdom from the Torah is acquired in 48 ways.

In Chinese numerology, 48 is an auspicious number that stands for prosperity. Possibly the prosperity that will follow the unleashing of your creativity!

CONTENTS

Preface	xi
Acknowledgements	xv

PART A
1. But I'm not creative! — 3
2. So, what exactly is creativity? — 11
3. A brief history of creativity — 16
4. Creative heroes from history — 20
5. History to neurology — 27
6. The path to creativity — 34
7. Mindful or mind full? — 43
8. More brainy stuff — 49
9. The 10 laws of creativity — 56
10. Manifesting your mantra — 59

PART B
11. The Six-Day Boot Camp — 66
12. Week 1: Dealing with Our Fear of Evaluation — 85
13. WEEK 2: Coping with Our Fear of Failure — 111
14. WEEK 3: Working with the Limitations of Rules — 125
15. Week 4: Embracing the Pain of Comparisons — 135
16. Week 5: Understanding the Myth of Talent — 143
17. Week 6: Acknowledging Our Limited Knowledge — 157

Epilogue	169
About the Author	171

PREFACE

The central idea of this book was born with me. At least, that's how I like to think of it!

The notion that I, like everyone else, was born creative and could stir up my creativity was always in my mind, trying to find newer dimensions as it expanded, grew and pushed outwards, becoming fuller and fuller. Initially, it struggled to express itself through my confused study choices as I first picked science and then arts. It probably found more meaning at work as I gravitated towards creative professions. Later, my creativity became a part of self-experimentation as I tried to write a book (not this one). During that period, it became such an overwhelming force that it decided to come out of me in the form of this book.

For someone with little formal schooling, my creativity always found unique expression. Looking back, connecting the dots, I see it was always there. My creativity began to develop with voracious reading, constant storytelling, imaginary conversations, setting up competitions between clouds in the sky and seeing trilogies play out in ant colonies in the garden. Music, language and literature along with sport, motorbikes and long hair were the more typical manifestations during my childhood and teenage years. My experiments in my 20s with methods of mind control and uncovering deeper levels of consciousness possibly also shaped my subsequent career choices and led me into design-related professions. Many years later, mindfulness or present moment awareness came knocking. And, along with that came many 'ahas'!

Some years ago, when I was working at IDEO, I tried to write a novel about a guy's journey to self-discovery. All I discovered was that writing a book was hard. Incredibly hard! As I tried to find ways to be more creative, I kept going back to my mindfulness practices. One day, I realised what was happening—something far bigger than the book I was attempting to write was trying to manifest through me. So, I set up a parallel track and started recording all my experiences and ideas. I also started researching and speaking to people individually and at forums about the idea that creativity is inherent in all of us and the really creative ones are those who have found ways to keep it alive, or uncovering it when needed. I even set up a separate table to write this book! What you are holding in your hands right now is the result of what occurred over the next few years.

Along the way, I've not only been able to test these exercises on myself and people I have taught, but also refine them to make them more effective and fun.

So, is this a textbook? Or is it a manual?

Whatever you call it, this is not something you read and put away on your bookshelf. While this book is no treatise on anything, it is meant to be your guide, friend, companion and a canvas for the journey to rediscover your creative self. Carry it with you, make notes, record your thoughts, ideate, scribble and treat it like an extension of your personality because that is exactly what it is!

This book is divided into Part A and Part B. Read Part A completely and then start the programme outlined in Part B. However, while in Part A, keep diving into certain exercises in Part B that you are advised to do.

As you read and work with this book, many changes will be set in motion. Some will be visible, many invisible. You do not have to believe this right now. Simply suspend judgement, observe and note the process as it unravels, for when you look back, you will have tracked your own creative rebirthing.

ACKNOWLEDGEMENTS

The universe and all the spiritually advanced beings who conspired to make me take this journey and manifest this idea through me.

My parents, Natesan Krishnaswamy and Lalitha Krishnaswamy for being relentless writers. In pursuing their purpose with such passion, they left me with no choice but to be inspired.

All the immensely creative people I have been fortunate to work and play with, for (knowingly and unknowingly) allowing me to look a little deeper into them.

Sheetal, for being my invaluable sounding board and helper.

Anamika, for bringing my visions to life with her illustrations in this book.

Supriya, for supporting my years of preparation, immersion, incubation and illumination, not to mention putting up with all the days of frustration!

Friends, family, students and colleagues for your conviction in the idea, your belief that I could do it and your support when I actually did.

Finally, as form follows function, I thank my publishers for giving this the form it has.

PART A

1. BUT I'M NOT CREATIVE!

'Gosh, I wish I was more creative!' Most of us have heard this statement and many of us have said it sometimes. Almost all of us have experienced it, at least on a few occasions. And those who say they have never felt this way, well, they probably lie.

Creativity is often thought of as a mysterious and wonderful gift that the right-brained and talented other half of the population has. Writers, painters, sculptors, poets, designers and such are widely considered creative, while us ordinary folks like software engineers, bankers, lawyers, business managers, taxi drivers and cooks are not. But bankers and taxi drivers can be extremely creative. Just ask someone who lives in New York, London, Hong Kong or Mumbai!

Creativity is also often thought to be genetic. You are either born with it or you are not. But ask any child to create, and whether it's a painting, sand castle or consistently dreaming up impossible worlds inside a discarded cardboard carton or makeshift quilt tent, he or she has no hesitation jumping in and getting swept away by the beautiful energy of creating!

Why does this happen so easily? How is it that a child does not seem to face any barriers to being creative?

> *Every child is an artist. The problem is staying an artist when you grow up.*
>
> Pablo Picasso

More importantly, what on earth happens after childhood? Why have so many of us been unable to tap into the creativity we had as children? Is it the fault of education? Does it suppress creativity? Does education truly prepare us for anything apart from a career?

Are teachers afraid of creativity? Who, then, cultivates our creative skills that allow us to derive the most out of our lives, our relationships? To get wealthy? Or build a business that impacts the world in a great way?

> *It's a miracle that curiosity survives formal education.*
>
> Albert Einstein

Perhaps it's society; with all its norms, expectations and cultural biases, it kills creativity at some point in our adult lives.

Or, is it maybe our professions? Our workplaces, where employers force us behind desks and make us do things we never want to do or are meant to do? Before you thump your desk in agreement, consider this: An oft-quoted IBM study[1] of over 1,500 CEOs from 60 countries and 33 industries found that CEOs rate creativity as the most

---

1 https://www.ibm.com/news/ca/en/2010/05/20/v384864m81427w34.html

important skill in today's volatile, uncertain, complex and ambiguous world. Strange. Why would they rate creativity so highly if they indeed are responsible for its loss in the first place?

In another survey across three continents by Adobe Systems,[2] only 25 per cent of the 5,000 polled felt they were living up to their creative potential. So, is the loss of creativity our own failing? A loss caused by fear of failure, our judgemental nature, the rules we create to govern our thinking and our lives, and the need to do the logical and sensible thing? Perhaps it has something to do with the fact that we have allowed ourselves to be conformed into comfortable moulds. Maybe, it's a loss caused by our need for standards, and the consequent adhering to, and judging or being judged by them.

The loss of creativity could also be a mental dysfunction. Does it go unrecognised because it has become the new normal?

If you feel all these factors have contributed in different degrees to the loss of your creativity, I agree with you. And if you believe that creative moments are vital in life—in work, relationships, families, society—you are probably taking the first step towards introducing the power of creativity in your own life.

A number of studies have been conducted on creativity, including studies of the brain, and many good books have been written on the subject. All point to the fact that creativity can be revived through various methods.

So, how do we expand our mind and unleash our creative potential to achieve all that we are meant to in a lifetime? How do we hack our brain to do our bidding and solve problems in amazingly creative ways?

---

2 https://www.adobe.com/aboutadobe/pressroom/pressreleases/201204/042312AdobeGlobalCreativityStudy.html

FINDING MY CREATIVITY IS A-PEELING!

Let's start with two things that impact the way we see the world and consequently, the way we live:

1. **The hardware or our beliefs.** These are mostly picked up during our growing years and remain fairly static even as everything around us changes. Some psychologists say that around 70 per cent of these beliefs are disempowering. Imagine a computer from the 1980s, 1990s, or even 10 years ago operating in today's hi-tech environment without an upgrade! A RAM built during those years in a machine that's operating in the artificial intelligence age! Likewise,

most of us operate on beliefs we probably picked up as children and never changed. Maybe one of those beliefs was formed when you were told you were not creative.
2. **Our software or our life systems.** Life systems are the way we live, the way we exercise our bodies and our minds, how we conduct our relationships, etc. And like software runs on hardware, your life systems run on your beliefs. So, maybe the way you live is based on the belief that you are not creative.

We always strive to upgrade our computers' systems to newer versions, if not the latest ones. But have you ever done that to your thinking? When was the last time you refreshed your Thoughts App? Most people never do. Are you still surprised the system hangs?

What if there is a powerful way to kick-start your unlimited human potential? A way to upgrade your hardware and software, a super-method by which your creative spirit could be revived? Benefits like improved concentration, better health and greater well-being are add-ons?

What if I told you that with adequate practise, this method could even make fairly impossible things happen. (In my case, it was my mother-in-law getting to like me!) It's like a buy-one-get-two-free deal!

Creative confidence is like a muscle—it can be strengthened and nurtured through effort and experience.

Tom and David Kelly of IDEO,
in their wonderful book *Creative Confidence*

Modern English calls this secret mindfulness, and on this journey, you'll see how it works. Come, upgrade your life! You will find new states of being you didn't even know existed.

The origins of mindfulness can be traced to meditation and other ancient contemplative disciplines. Buddhist meditation, in particular, is probably what has most inspired the practices that are today defined as mindfulness.

English Lesson 1

Do you remember learning in grammar class that adding 'ness' to a word makes it a noun? By that definition, mindful*ness* has to be a thing. For me, it is a state of energy.

English Lesson 2

Mindfulness is the opposite of mindlessness, where mindless represents an autopilot mode in which we operate in a conditioned manner governed by rules and routines and are trapped in rigid mindsets to make fewer mistakes. Of course, all this occurs while being completely oblivious to the present moment.

But what does being aware of the present moment have to do with our ability to become creative problem-solving ninjas?

Aha! Well, *that's* what this book is all about.

This book is designed to be read and worked on at the same time. You will keep diving into Part B while reading Part A.

Note: Gift yourself a creativity journal to accompany your reading. You are going to want to track your progress. Writing about your experiences and thoughts during your reading of this book and reflecting on them as you go along, or even after you are done with your first complete reading, will help you capture your journey and strengthen the process. You will also be using the journal during many of the exercises in Part B.

Excited? Feel like getting a taste of things already?

Try the exercise in Part B called 'Getting to Ness' on page 77.

2. SO, WHAT EXACTLY IS CREATIVITY?

Creativity is allowing yourself to make mistakes. Art is knowing which ones to keep.

Scott Adams

There are many definitions of creativity, and rightfully so. After all, it is creativity we are defining! They range from scientifically precise explanations to more literary, artistic, spiritual and downright funny descriptions.

According to Wikipedia, creativity is a phenomenon whereby something new and somehow valuable is formed. The created item may be intangible (such as an idea, a scientific theory, a musical composition or a joke) or an original physical object (such as an invention, a literary work or a painting).

Steve Jobs, one of the most creative people the world has seen over the past two decades, famously said, 'Creativity is just connecting things. When you ask creative people how they did something, they feel a little guilty because they didn't really do it, they just saw something. It seemed obvious to them after a while.'[3]

David and Tom Kelly in *Creative Confidence* say, 'We think of creativity as using your imagination to create something new in the world.'

Spiritual guru Osho says, 'To be creative means to be in love with life. You can be creative only if you love life enough that you want to enhance its beauty, you want to bring a little more music to it, a little more poetry to it, a little more dance to it.'[4]

> When an emotion arises, release it through your body in the form of any exercise. Second, learn to be creative. You are all without creativity.
>
> Last night, I was talking about how in the old days each village had a cobbler, and whenever somebody wore his shoes the cobbler would say with pride, 'I have made them.' It was an artist's pride. Another man would make wheels for the carts, and with pride he too would say, 'They have been made by me.'
>
> In these times you have lost the pleasure from creating—there is not much left that is made by human hands. You don't create anything. The way the world is right now, soon there will be nothing left that has been made by human hands. And the joy one used to get from creating something has disappeared. If that is destroyed, what will happen to all this energy? It will become destructive. Naturally, energy has to move in some direction, either towards destruction or towards creativity.

---

3 https://www.brainyquote.com/quotes/steve_jobs_416925
4 https://www.goodreads.com/quotes/377058-to-be-creative-means-to-be-in-love-with-life

Learn to lead a creative life. Creativity means that you do something solely for the joy it gives you. You can sculpt, write a song, sing a song, play the sitar—it does not matter what you do, but do it only for pleasure and not as a profession. Do something in life which is only for pleasure, something which is not your profession. Then all the destructive energy will be transformed and will become creative.

I have asked you to redirect your emotions, and to give this ordinary life a creative direction. Don't worry, you can just make a garden around your house and love the plants and take pleasure in them. You don't have to do much—polish a stone and make a statue out of it! Every intelligent man needs to do something creative besides his means of livelihood. Someone who gives no time to creativity will be troubled, and he will ruin his own life.

You can write a small song—you don't have to do much. Go to a hospital and give flowers to the sick. If you see a beggar on the road, give him a hug. Do something creative, which is only for your pleasure, in which you don't have to give anything and you don't have to take anything; the act itself is your joy.

So, choose an activity in your life, which is only for your pleasure. Direct all your energy towards it, and then there will be no destructive energy left. The more creative you are, the more your anger will disappear. Anger is the sign of an uncreative person.

The Path of Meditation
Courtesy: Osho International

> *Creativity is intelligence having fun.*
>
> Albert Einstein

As for me, I think creativity is actually an energy.

For most of my career, I have been in creative professions and surrounded by creative types. Many years ago, I even tried dressing like one of them, although I never summoned the courage to grow a ponytail to cement my creative stature.

At IDEO, I had the privilege of working alongside some of the most creative people on the planet. I've felt the energy these people carry with them. It's like an aura, although you have to look beyond what's visible to see it. If you have been in a room full of creative people brainstorming, you have certainly felt the buzz. There is a lot of fun and laughter. People constantly come up with ideas (many of them crazy!) without the fear of being judged, toss them around, build on them and collaborate. Soon, ideas start coming together and growing in this environment of playfulness.

Creativity is a state of energy. One that allows you to connect with both the familiar and unfamiliar areas of life from a fresh perspective and in doing so, facilitates the birth of something unique.

Many a time, I've seen the oh-so-serious business executive or CEO squirm in discomfort or look on disdainfully at this not-so-serious process, only to be left stunned by how quickly creative energy bubbles up to solve problems.

Creativity—an energy? Seriously?

If that's what you are thinking, here is an exercise that should help you.

First, we identify the state of energy. We learn to recognise it. Then slowly, with practise, you will also be able to call upon it at will. It's akin to the good old genie in the bottle who comes to do your bidding and creatively solves your problems!

Sounds unbelievable? For now, take my word for it. You will soon see how some of the most creative minds in history discovered this secret and made it work for them.

In every work of genius, we recognise our own rejected thoughts.

Ralph Waldo Emerson

Try the exercise in Part B called 'Colouring' on page 100.
In your creativity journal, write a few lines about the experience. Some prompts you may use: How long did you take? Did you do it fast? Or slow? How did it feel? Was there a sense of impatience? A sense of wanting to complete the task? What else did you notice?

3. A BRIEF HISTORY OF CREATIVITY

The word 'create' comes from the Greek word 'creo', which means to make, and it appears in English only around the fourteenth century, to indicate divine creation. Creativity was thus long seen as the sole privilege of God, and human beings were not seen as capable of creating something new except as an expression of God's work.

> *Is man one of God's blunders, or is God one of man's blunders?*
>
> Friedrich Nietzsche

Unsurprisingly, it is commonly argued that the notion of creativity originated in Western culture through Christianity. A number of Western studies say that more ancient cultures like those of China and India lacked the concept of creativity.

Some Western studies have even stated that a culture like Greece did not have creativity. This may be because when Plato was asked in *The Republic*, 'Will we say, of a painter, that he makes something?', he famously said, 'Certainly not, he merely imitates.' But his student, Aristotle, said, 'No, man is creative!' Talk about student-teacher friction!

In *Creative Confidence*, David and Tom Kelly share a fascinating insight they acquired from Geshe Thupten Jinpa, the Dalai Lama's chief English translator, on the nature of creativity. 'Jinpa pointed out that there is no word in the Tibetan language for creativity or being creative. The closest translation is natural. In other words, if you want to be more creative, you just have to be more natural.'

Interestingly, we also have from the *Book of Genesis*: 'And God made man in his own image.' So I ask you, if God was creative, and God made man in his own image, does simple deductive logic not suggest that man is also creative? If A = B and B = C, then A = C.

Confusing? Wait. There is hope! Around the Renaissance, there began a movement, which suggested creativity could also be an act of man. And while slow, it gained traction over the next few centuries.

Phew! Thank God for revolutions!

By the eighteenth century, creativity was finding separate mention and being linked with imagination, and there were even attempts to separate it from talent (originally a measure of weight and currency used by Greeks and Romans but going on to mean a natural aptitude or skill).

However, creativity was first studied only in the nineteenth century. Since then, a number of concepts have emerged around it, and there are many studies that explore the link between creativity and disciplines like philosophy, technology, science, linguistics, business, art and songwriting.

Today, it is accepted in virtually every aspect of our lives. We have creativity in art, science, medicine, philosophy, technology, language, cooking, fashion, construction, law, finance and education. And, as you can see from this book, even a random guy like me can get creative!

4. CREATIVE HEROES FROM HISTORY

Wow! You buy a book on creativity and get history lessons too! Pretty cool, isn't it?

Let's first meet the man whose name has come to symbolise smartness. The one man who is probably quoted most often on diverse topics. The man who said, 'I very rarely think in words at all. A thought comes, and I may try to express it in words afterwards.'

Albert Einstein

Many of Einstein's biographies state that he actually found inspiration for the theory of special relativity in a dream he had as a teenager.

In it, Einstein was walking across a field where a herd of cows was huddled near an electric fence. On the other end of the field was the farmer. Einstein saw the farmer suddenly switch on the electricity and the cows jumped back in shock (what kind of a farmer would risk electrocuting his cows?). Einstein approached the farmer and recounted that he saw all the cows jumping back in shock, but the farmer said he saw them jumping back one by one!

Most kids would have found this funny and probably tried this to emulate it while playing (I think that's where the Mexican wave originated from), but not Einstein! Instead, it inspired him to theorise that things seem different based on where you stand, because of the time it takes for light to travel that distance, i.e., the theory of special relativity.

So, one of humanity's most significant scientific discoveries was inspired by a dream in which a farmer got his cows to do the Mexican wave!

Friedrich August Kekulé

Benzene, as most people know, is a pretty important chemical. Its formula is C_6H_6, which means it has six carbon atoms and six hydrogen atoms, which is why it is cleverly called a hydrocarbon.

Benzene is one of the natural constituents of crude oil and an elementary petrochemical. We use loads of it to make stuff like nylon, rubber, lubricants, dyes, detergents, drugs, explosives and pesticides.

For years, scientists including Kekulé had struggled with the nomenclature of benzene. Then, one day, as Kekulé sat half asleep in his armchair by the fireplace, he saw a snake trying to eat its own tail in the sparks leaping out of the fire. Most people would have jumped up with a scream and ran, but Kekulé wrote down the ring-like chemical structure of benzene instead.

Salvador Dali

If you were beginning to think that discoveries in dreams or dream-like states occur only among scientists, you're wrong. Surrealist master Dali had fine-tuned the channelling of dreams into art.

He would sit in a comfortable chair, drape his hand over the armrest holding a spoon and place a plate just below it.

Eventually, a sleep-like state would wash over him and all kinds of images would float into his mind. At the point where he lapsed into actual sleep, the spoon would fall from his hand onto the plate, and the resulting clang would wake him up. Then, he would quickly capture the surreal images through art.

I can think of a few people who fall asleep so quickly that they wouldn't hear a clap of thunder, leave alone a spoon falling on a plate. Clearly, they need another method to capture their dreams!

James Cameron

Arnold Schwarzenegger must surely have thanked James Cameron's wild dream for giving him the role of a lifetime! Cameron thought up *The Terminator* thanks to a dream (more like a nightmare I'd imagine!) about a huge fire, and a robot emerging from it with knives for hands. In the movie, Sarah Connor, played by Linda Hamilton, has visions of impending doom that would bring the human race to the brink of extinction. It has a lot of dreamlike imagery and even the way Model T-800 moves was supposedly inspired by the dream.

The science fiction franchise has grossed billions of dollars.

Wolfgang Amadeus Mozart

Mozart has stated that entire symphonies came to him in dreams. He also sketched drafts of his music as they came to him. In a letter that Mozart wrote to his father Leopold, he discussed his work in Munich on the opera *Idomeneo* (30 December 1780) and distinguished 'composed' from 'written': 'I must finish [writing this letter] now, because I've got to write at breakneck speed—everything is composed—but not written yet.'

Now you're probably beginning to think, 'Ah, I get it. This is about dozing my way to creativity.'

Close, but not exactly!

George de Mestral

In 1948, de Mestral, a Swiss engineer and amateur inventor, returned home from a hunting trip with his dog and over a cup of tea, found his pants and the dog's fur covered in burrs. Upon examining closely under a microscope, de Mestral found that these seed sacs had tiny hooks to cling to the minute loops of the fabric. Velour, a kind of velvety fabric used in upholstery and heavy clothing, had combined with crochet or the crooked knitting needle to form Velcro! De Mestral patented the idea, formed Velcro Companies and a multimillion-dollar industry was born. People may have accused him of ripping off the idea from nature, but this is a classic example of a great idea that stuck.

And the list goes on.

History is full of examples of men and women who've experienced such breakthrough creative moments. I'm sure you are beginning to see a pattern in these examples. They have one thing in common—all these 'aha' moments happened when the person was in a relaxed state of mind.

But a key thing to also note is that many of them were focused on a particular problem or topic or idea they were trying to solve. In fact, you could say they were obsessed with it. Einstein and Kekulé had been consumed by their problems for years before they cracked the answers. Dali thought of nothing but creating new things, whether it was painting or writing, and Cameron breathed movies as much as Mozart heard music every moment of his life.

So, here is my big aha!

Creative energy flows best when you are relaxed but not lax. When you are intense but not tense.

Jiddu Krishnamurti says it beautifully in *Education and the Significance of Life*:

'To be creative is not merely to produce poems, or statues, or children; it is to be in that state in which truth can come into being. Truth comes into being when there is complete cessation of thought; and thought ceases only when the self is absent, when the mind has ceased to create, that is, when it is no longer caught in its own pursuits. When the mind is utterly still without being forced or trained into quiescence, when it is silent because the self is inactive, then there is creation.'

Just when you thought it was all about taking naps and relaxing, it's time to work that brain a bit!
Try the exercise in Part B called 'Body Scan' on page 67.

5. HISTORY TO NEUROLOGY

I'm sure you have figured it out by now that I'm a pretty earnest guy. I really want this book to give you your money's worth. So, I figured I'd throw in a tiny lesson in neuroscience as well.

It's more like neuroscience for dummies. Not that you are dumb. You wouldn't have bought this book otherwise! But there's just some basic information about the brain you need before you again jump up and say, 'Aha! I get it. Now give me the real stuff.'

While manuscripts suggest the Egyptians knew about brain damage as early as 1700 BC, traditionally, the study of the brain was a branch of biology. Neuroscience is a relatively new field—the International Brain Research Organization was formed only in 1961.

Now for the brainy bit. The brain is really cool because it does pretty amazing stuff. It helps you see, sense things like heat, cold, etc., and salivate when you see or smell your favourite food. It makes you feel emotions like love, joy and fear, and prompts you to run from danger. It contemplates beauty, philosophy, God and other abstract concepts. Why, it is even aware of how it contemplates and helps man study itself!

While the brain is small enough to fit in the palm of your hand and weighs just around 1,300 to 1,400 grams, it consumes 20 per cent of the energy the body generates (around 25 watts, enough to power a small light bulb). It's made up mostly of fat and water and has around 100 billion neurons and no nerves.

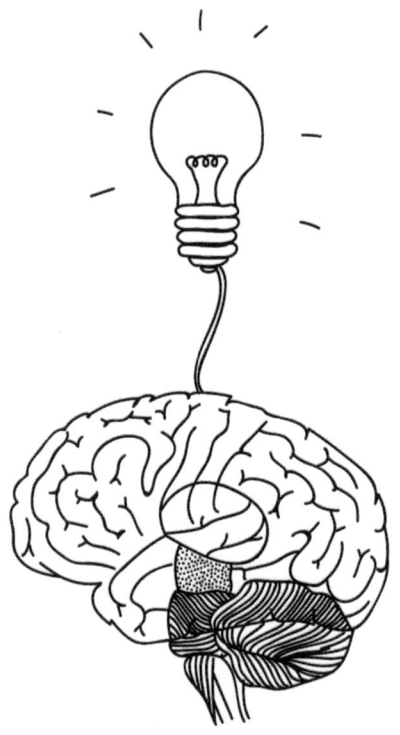

The brain has three parts—lower brain, cerebellum and higher brain or cerebrum. The lower brain receives signals from our five senses and processes them. It is responsible for our survival, so when it perceives a threat to survival (in my case, my mother in-law), it puts us in fight, flight or freeze mode. The cerebellum coordinates movement, while the cerebrum helps us experience emotions, connect the dots and come up with creative ideas. It is also responsible for language and math skills, and constitutes almost 75 per cent of the brain by size.

Like muscles, the brain grows with exercise. For example, London's taxi drivers, who need to memorise maps of the entire city to earn a licence, have an enlarged hippocampus—the memory region—as shown in the MRIs. This feature of the brain is called neuroplasticity.

Intuitively and etymologically, the word neuroplasticity suggests the ability of neurons to change themselves. That is a simple yet close-enough definition of what is an extremely complex scientific process! Neuroplasticity or brain plasticity is the way the brain changes in response to experience. It refers to alterations in synapses and/or other aspects of neurons that affect how information is processed and transmitted in the nervous system.

Neuroplasticity is a complex phenomenon that involves several processes. Simplistically speaking, neurons either grow stronger or weaker at the synaptic level (the junction between two nerve cells) or at a structural level. Potentiation occurs when parts or chains of neurons grow stronger due to more use, while depression signifies their weakening due to disuse or underuse. Both processes go hand in hand, with neurons either sprouting or pruning structurally, while at the synaptic level, it relates to the amount of neurotransmitters released and the volume of information flowing between neurons.

Neuroplasticity is continuous as one learns and the brain develops. In a sense, it's a built-in mechanism in the brain for fine-tuning efficiency. Remember neuropsychologist Donald Hebb's clever phrase, 'Neurons that fire together, wire together.'[5]

While the term neuroplasticity has been in use for a fairly long time, until around the 1970s, neuroscientists believed that the brain's structure and function were essentially fixed throughout adulthood. Maybe this is where the adage—you can't teach an old dog new tricks—arose. It is only recently that the element of plasticity has been researched well, and mounting evidence suggests that old dogs can, in fact, learn new tricks. Good news for folks like me!

Among the neuroscientific studies that specifically look at creativity, Dr Nancy Andreasen's work is seminal. In 2000, the then US president Bill Clinton awarded Dr Andreasen, the world-leading creativity expert, the National Medal of Science, the country's highest honour for scientific achievement.

Dr Andreasen has studied different types of creativity. She looks at the neural basis for creativity, exploring creative traits in a group of creative people—not just any group, but one made up of creative geniuses!

'The capacity to develop original or novel ideas or to produce novel, beautiful and useful artifacts is perhaps the most important cognitive trait that human beings possess,' she has said. 'However, it has rarely been studied

---

5   https://en.wikipedia.org/wiki/Hebbian_theory

scientifically. Although investigators have attempted to develop ways to study the creative process using creativity tests, these methods are not well-supported in terms of either face or predictive validity. The best work to date has been based on the case study method, through which creative people are studied using interviews about their work habits and sources of insight. These studies have also examined the relationship between intelligence and creativity. This work indicates that the creative process depends heavily on intuition and flashes of insight rather than analytic processes. It also indicates that being highly creative is not equivalent to having a high IQ; the average IQ in creative people is around 120. People with high IQs (e.g. 140 range) are not necessarily creative.'[6]

Referring to the subjects in her study, she wrote in the article 'Secrets of the Creative Brain' in *The Atlantic*'s July/August 2014 issue, 'My individual jewels so far include, among others, the film-maker George Lucas, the mathematician and Fields Medallist William Thurston, the Pulitzer Prize–winning novelist Jane Smiley, and six Nobel laureates from the fields of chemistry, physics, and physiology or medicine. Because winners of major awards are typically older, and because I wanted to include some younger people, I've also recruited winners of the National Institutes of Health Pioneer Award and other prizes in the arts.'

That's some creative firepower!

Dr Andreasen also explains the methods she has employed to conduct her study: 'They are studied by obtaining structural and functional magnetic resonance scans of their brains using equipment in the Department of Radiology at the Carver College of Medicine. They are also interviewed by me, using an individualised

---

[6] http://www.nancyandreasen.com/id2.html

interview that explores their work habits and the way they get their creative ideas. Their personal and family histories are also reviewed. Finally, they are assessed with a group of standard neurocognitive tests. The study takes about one-and-a-half days. All subjects are able to review and ask questions about their own brain images.' Dr Andreasen's subjects receive a booklet describing their individual brain characteristics, a model of their brain reconstructed from the scans and a CD containing their brain images, which they can review later or share with their physicians.

Pretty comprehensive study that!

In the article, Dr Andreasen states, 'Almost all of my subjects confirmed that when eureka moments occur, they tend to be precipitated by long periods of preparation and incubation, and strike when the mind is relaxed—during that state we called REST (Random Episodic Silent Thought). "A lot of it happens when you are doing one thing and you're not thinking about what your mind is doing," one of the artists in my study told me. "I'm either watching television, I'm reading a book, and I make a connection… It may have nothing to do with what I am doing, but somehow or the other, you see something or hear something or do something, and it pops that connection together." Many subjects mentioned lighting on ideas while showering, driving, or exercising. One described a more unusual regimen involving an afternoon nap: "It's during this nap that I get a lot of my work done. I find that when the ideas come to me, they come as I'm falling asleep, they come as I'm waking up, they come if I'm sitting in the tub. I don't normally take baths, but sometimes I'll just go in there and have a think".'

Put all this down for an unscientific brain like mine and two things stand out:
1. The neocortex in the higher brain is responsible for creativity.
2. MRI studies show fairly conclusively that the neocortex lights up when a person is relaxed, like half asleep, or on a leisurely walk or in the shower.

It kind of sounds like a bandwidth thing to me. If the bandwidth is choked by the lower brain occupying itself with stress-causing stimuli (maybe a mother-in-law), information does not make it to the higher brain so it can come up with cool stuff.

Wow! History and neurology seem to be pointing in the same direction!

Try the exercise in Part B called 'Writing Meditation' on page 71.

6. THE PATH TO CREATIVITY

Well, it's not a straight one. But don't let that discourage you. History and science are providing reassuring evidence for us to take the journey to rediscover our creative selves!

Let's take a look at what our route might look like.

Early accounts of the creative process were provided by pioneering theorists such as Henri Poincaré, Graham Wallas and Max Wertheimer. In his work *Art of Thought* published in 1926, Wallas presented one of the first models of the creative process, explained in five stages:

Preparation: Preparatory work on a problem that focuses the individual's mind on the problem and explores the problem's dimensions.
Incubation: Where the problem is internalised into the unconscious mind and nothing appears externally to be happening.
Intimation: The creative person gets a feeling that a solution is on its way.
Illumination or insight: Where the creative idea bursts forth from its preconscious processing into conscious awareness.
Verification: Where the idea is consciously verified, elaborated and then applied.

There is also another school of thought that I call the Zen Model of Creative Problem Solving. It does not involve long periods of standing on one leg with eyes closed and meditating. It's something far easier—you just become one with the problem. When you do, the solution reveals itself to you.

Now, how on earth do you become one with the problem, you'll ask? Well, more will be revealed to you as you progress on your creative journey!

But, just in case you're freaking out about how to become one with the problem, here is the good news—there is another path to creativity. It builds on Wallas' well-established model and consists of the four basic stages of creativity:

1. **Preparation**
2. **Immersion**
3. **Incubation**
4. **Illumination**

These steps are non-linear and work more like a spiral or, at times, even a maze! You will circle through some of them again and again, each time at a different level as creative energy builds inside you and keeps pushing you towards your aha moment.

Expect steps 1 and 3 to bring along some frustration as well. You will go through peaks and valleys, and even come close to abandoning the journey and returning to the comfort of your old life. But there will be little rewards to keep you on track. Remember, now that you are on your way to the land of creativity, you need to stay the course and trust the process. Feelings of doubt, anxiety and frustration are normal, and it's never too late to start, so keep going!

Preparation

Understanding the problem is the first step. How often do we see someone rushing off to solve a problem without fully understanding it? Preparation begins with seeing the problem from multiple perspectives and opening up to everything that is relevant to it. Asking the right questions is crucial. You then gather a lot of information so that unusual connections can be made. This, in fact, is the bedrock of great creative ideas. Remember what Jobs said about creativity being connections between random dots?

Perhaps you immediately perceive problems as your conditioning dictates. Do you wonder what others will think if you think of it differently, or do you believe you already know the problem well and have a solution prepared?

Being receptive, listening and keeping an open mind are key to preparation.

> *Luck is what happens when preparation meets opportunity.*
>
> Seneca

Immersion

If preparation is the stage where you go broad and collect everything that might be of use to you in solving a problem, immersion is when you go deep. This stage is about acquiring domain-specific knowledge and attaining a high level of skill in the area the problem pertains to. Einstein and Kekulé were experts in their fields just as our other creative heroes. They had spent years gaining knowledge and immersing themselves in their area of passion.

Incubation

Incubation is the favourite stage for lazy guys like me. It's even better than illumination because once there is the aha, you have to do something about it. Incubation is where you can relax, like a hen sitting on her eggs or cows ruminating. Much of the grunt work is being done behind the scenes by the subconscious mind, while you sleep on it. Sounds nice, doesn't it?

But do not underestimate the importance of what's going on just because you can't see it. Your subconscious and unconscious minds store phenomenal amounts of information, including stuff you don't know you know! They make unpredictable connections that you can't even consciously imagine.

The answer may sometimes seem like it's coming to you in a dream or when you are in the shower. The problem and its circumstances will pop up periodically to remind you that it's still around. And just when it seems within grasp, it fades or bursts like a bubble in a moment of profound logic. Aargh!

Illumination

Illumination is the aha moment, the hero of the entire process, the part that gets all the glory. But it's not the end of the process. The aha needs to be translated into a course of action or something tangible.

And since we are on the subject of creativity, here's what the path might look like!

If this looks daunting, worry not! This is where a framework like design thinking can be really useful, helping to bring discipline to a seemingly confusing and complicated journey. It lays out a great set of fairly simple behaviours that anyone can follow to enhance their creativity.

People talk these days about the world being volatile, uncertain, complex and ambiguous, and here is also where design thinking can become a much-needed beacon of creative light.

> Developed originally by IDEO founder David Kelley, design thinking is defined as 'a human-centred approach to innovation that draws from the designer's toolkit to integrate the needs of people, the possibilities of technology, and the requirements for business success'.
> *Forbes*

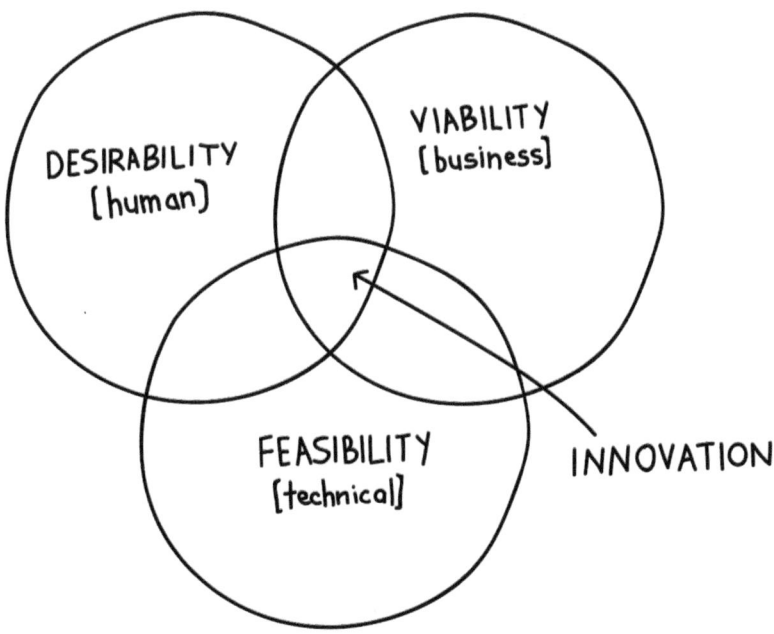

Here is a five-step process to describe design thinking:

Look closely. This process is actually pointing to interconnected behaviours that design thinkers exhibit. It is a pattern that is asked of you, and in demonstrating these behaviours, you can become more creative.

On another note, economist Joseph Schumpeter gave us an interesting concept—creative destruction—where the old is disrupted by the new through a vision. He explains vision as an intuitive act that supplies direction and energy to analytical efforts. It allows things to be seen in a new light and in a way that is not to be found in the facts, methods and end results of the existing state of the science.

What Schumpeter's concept also suggests is that while there can be scientific frameworks and processes, there is a mysterious and intangible aspect that finally connects the dots and ignites creativity. What is that aspect? That is our Holy Grail.

On this search for the Holy Grail, this journey to rediscover and reignite your creative energy, you also need to be aware of a few enemies—the goblins of the creative world. They hide behind little bushes and rocks on your path and as you walk past, stick their feet out and trip you up. You may stumble and that is OK. You may even fall but do pick yourself up and keep going, for their victory comes only when you abandon your journey. But each time you overcome one of them, their overall energies also weaken!

There is one ancient secret these goblins are terrified of—mindfulness. When goblins inhabit your mind, mindfulness is like a bright light that shines on them, forcing them to come scuttling out of the darkest corners. Under this light, they lose their powers, grow weak, shrivel up and die. It is for this reason they plot to make you fail in your practice of mindfulness.

There is another important thing mindfulness does—it allows you to nurture internal wellsprings that nourish and feed not only design thinking behaviours, but even behaviours your boss, or mother-in-law, might demand of you.

So, while design thinking says, go forth and empathise, mindfulness opens up the fountainheads of compassion, warmth and affinity that allow you to empathise. When design thinking urges you to define and ideate, mindfulness gives you the clarity and open mindedness you need to do so, successfully.

Finally, when all the diehard fans of design thinking (including me) rush to prototype, fail quickly, learn from failure, test and iterate stages, mindfulness provides the optimism, resilience and the emotional intelligence to persevere.

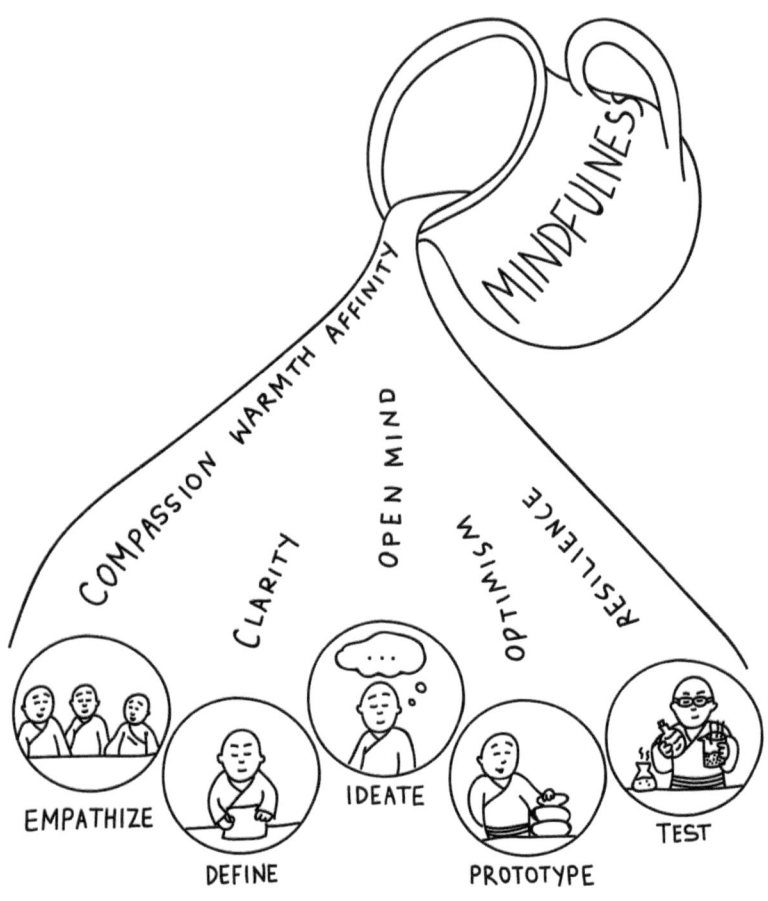

I will also tell you that mindfulness helps you to stay in the moment, listen deeply, ask the right questions and keep calm under pressure.

Imagine! Creativity without the stress and sweat. No tearing your hair out. Only a beatific smile!

7. MINDFUL OR MIND FULL?

Once upon a time, there was a guy who used to practise some yoga and a little meditation. He was a regular person, and like most regular people, he struggled to sit in one place and meditate for long periods of time. One day, he chanced upon a book by Zen Master Thich Nhat Hanh and after reading it a few times, he thought that maybe, just maybe, he did not have to sit in one place anymore to meditate. Aha! He began to teach himself mindfulness. Eventually, many years and many gurus later, he went to the Zen Master's monastery to elevate his practice and maybe even become a teacher. He secretly hoped to find enlightenment along the way.

A lot of practise and many, many moons later, he realised that nothing resembling enlightenment was going to happen. But something even more wonderful was happening—he was realising that mindfulness was not about getting someplace or becoming something, it was about simply being wherever he was, but in a more complete way. Mindfulness was the seed and also the fruit; the journey and also the destination.

If you haven't guessed already, the regular guy is me, and while the story may seem heroic, it was full of failures.

I, initially, called myself a loser every time my mind wandered, doubted my capabilities and had phases of going back to autopilot and mindless ways. But parallelly, through my formal and informal practise every day, an underlying ability was developing—the awareness that I was calling myself a loser, doubting my abilities or slipping into autopilot mode. The awareness of awareness. Didn't I tell you the brain is a pretty cool thing?

To check how mindful you are, answer yes or no to the following questions. Do this before turning the page.

1. I am a master of multitasking and I can do a number of things at the same time without focusing on any one thing.
   YES/NO
2. I am a tech and social media whiz and I operate on four to five different platforms at any given point in time.
   YES/NO
3. I am like a cool automatic car and I zip through life without paying attention to most things around me.
   YES/NO
4. I can sit and just lose myself in thoughts and feelings.
   YES/NO
5. I eat without being aware of it and I can read, watch TV, check emails or talk to someone on the phone while at it. I can even eat when I am driving.
   YES/NO
6. I love thinking about the past and the future.
   YES/NO
7. When someone is talking to me, I can easily do a couple of other things like check my phone or reply to an email or text.
   YES/NO
8. When someone is speaking to me, I am so smart that I can complete their sentence for them or answer their question even before they finish asking it.
   YES/NO
9. I can go through things without paying much attention to them.
   YES/NO
10. I often find myself rushing from one thing to another.
    YES/NO

If you have said yes to most of these, congratulations! You, like I did, represent exactly what mindfulness is not!

Now that you know what mindfulness is not, let's take a deeper look at what mindfulness is.

Mindfulness has its roots in ancient contemplative practices, which have been refined and adapted in many ways over the centuries. The term mindfulness is unfortunately often misunderstood, as it appears to suggest that the mind is full. Some traditions use it as a term for noticing when the mind wanders. So, then, mindfulness could well be part of a sequence of attention, then mind wandering, then the moment of noticing the wandering and finally, the return to the point of attention.

The concept of mindfulness could also be traced to the Pali term 'sati' and its Sanskrit counterpart 'smriti'.

Sati is literally memory, but used with reference to the constantly repeated phrase mindful and thoughtful (sato sampajâno), meaning activity of mind and constant presence of mind, which is one of the duties most frequently inculcated in a good Buddhist.

Another interpretation of mindfulness is the awareness of whatever happens in our experience without judging or reacting to it.

Mindfulness is the energy of being aware and awake to the present moment. It is the continuous practice of touching life deeply in every moment of daily life. To be mindful is to be truly alive, present, and at one with the body and mind in harmony while we wash the dishes, drive the car or take our morning shower.

Thich Nhat Hanh

Mindfulness is paying attention in a particular way on purpose, in the present moment and non-judgementally.

Jon Kabat-Zinn

Mindfulness means paying attention to what's happening in the presnt moment in the mind, body and external environment, with an attitude of curiosity and kindness.

Mindful Nation UK Report, 2015

Recently, I had a conversation with some friends who wondered if carpe diem or the example of a sniper ready to shoot could denote mindfulness. The sniper would be hyper-aware and attentive, and if his mind wandered, he would bring it back on his target, they said. But what is missing for the sniper, according to me, is compassion, warmth and a non-judgemental state of accepting the existence of the target without the need to destroy it. This openness to each moment without judgement is what allows us to deal with worry, anxiety, fear and consequent stress. This—non-judgemental present moment awareness—is really what mindfulness is all about.

However, since we're keeping everything simple in this book, let us accept there is no single word in English that is a perfect translation of sati. English does have an interesting word, though, which is not often used when we speak of mindfulness, but suggests something similar—anoesis, a state of mind consisting of pure sensation or emotion without cognition.

> Once, the Buddha was walking from one town to another with a few followers. This was in the initial days. While they were travelling, they happened to come by a lake. They stopped and the Buddha told one of his disciples, 'I am thirsty. Do get me some water.'
>
> The disciple walked to the lake and when he reached it, he noticed people washing clothes in the water and a bullock cart crossing through. The water became muddy and turbid, so the disciple thought, 'How can I give this muddy water to the Buddha to drink?' He came back and told the Buddha, 'The lake's water is very muddy. I don't think it is fit to drink.'
>
> After about half an hour, the Buddha again asked the same disciple to return to the lake and get him water to drink. The disciple obediently went and found that the water had cleared. The mud had settled, so he filled a pot and brought it to the Buddha.
>
> The Buddha looked at the water, and then at the disciple, and said, 'Look at what you did to make the water clean. You let it be and the mud settled on its own. Your mind is also like this. When it is disturbed, let it be. Give it a little time. It will settle down on its own. You don't have to make an effort to calm it. It will happen. It is effortless.'
>
> What did the Buddha emphasise? He said, 'It is effortless.' Attaining peace of mind is not a strenuous job, it is an effortless process. When there is peace inside you, it is reflected on the outside. It spreads in the environment, such that people around you feel that peace and grace.

We all have moments of mindfulness. Do you remember intently listening to your favourite song for a few moments with your full being? Taking a bite of your favourite dish and going 'mmmmmm', possibly closing your eyes? Coming upon a wondrous natural sight that took your breath away or staring into the eyes of a baby or a loved one or an animal, and for a moment feeling an inexplicable connection but no thought?

These are all wonderful moments of mindfulness we experience in day-to-day life. There's only one tiny problem—they are too few and far between. What if there are simple exercises that would enable you to experience this energy or be in this state of 'ness' a lot more often? With enough practise, at all times? Woah! Wouldn't that be something?

It *is* possible! But be sure to read the fine print before you continue!

1. Mindfulness will not help you levitate. ☺
2. Mindfulness is not about religion.
3. Mindfulness will not remove pain.
4. Mindfulness is not about an empty mind.

8. MORE BRAINY STUFF

In Chapter 5, we took a look at what happens in the brain when creativity sparks. Now, let's examine some of the things that happen in the brain during the practice of mindfulness, so we can connect the dots even better.

If neuroscience is just 50 to 60 years old, the study of the neurological effects of mindfulness is even more recent. But there is an increasing number of studies that provide evidence of how mindfulness affects the brain's structure and functions. Some of these studies are more conclusive than others, but, in my opinion, there is enough to connect the dots. In fact, it would be accurate to say that there has been an explosion in the number of scientific studies on mindfulness over the past few years.

Neuroscience also offers evidence that while all contemplative practices have immediate and long-term benefits (depending on how many hours are spent on them), different kinds of meditation lead to a variety of mental habits. For example, researchers at the Max Planck Institute for Human Cognitive and Brain Sciences in Leipzig, Germany, had novices practising three different kinds of meditation for three months—focusing on breathing, generating loving kindness and monitoring thoughts. They found focusing on breathing calming (you, of course, know that already), but interestingly, the other two methods did not clearly demonstrate that they relaxed the body, possibly because they demand mental effort. Generating loving kindness to wish yourself and others well did lift the mood though.

Other fascinating findings point to the role of mindfulness in resilience, a key component of the creativity formula. Studies by eminent scientists like Richard Davidson and Carol Ryff have found that people with a stronger purpose in life recover more quickly from stressors induced in a lab. They also prove that with practise, positive states achieved during meditation can become lasting traits.[7]

Davidson's lab studied the brain of Yongey Mingyur Rinpoche, a Tibetan monk who had 62,000 hours of lifetime meditation. When he meditated on compassion, there was a massive surge in electrical activity in his brain. Functional MRI images reveal that during that period, his circuitry for empathy jumped 700 to 800 per cent over the baseline resting level! When he went under the scanner again four-and-a-half years later, they found his 41-year-old brain to be as young as that of a 33-year-old's. One can only imagine what the Rinpoche could do if he tried his hand at design thinking!

All this makes me think of meditation as something like sport, a gym for the mind.

In fact, we can think of meditation as a family of mental training practices that are designed to familiarise the practitioner with specific types of mental processes.

Like football builds strong legs, loving compassion meditation builds empathy. Just like all sports require a high level of general fitness, all meditation requires focused attention. This is exactly what breath awareness meditation does. It is the equivalent of basic physical fitness for any sport.

---

7   Anna-Lena Lumma et al., 'Is Meditation Always Relaxing? Investigating Heart Rate, Heart Rate Variability, Experienced Effort and Likeability During Training of Three Types of Meditation', *International Journal of Psychophysiology* 97 (2015): 38–45.

Here are a few more case studies of mindfulness meditation from a neuroscience perspective. Researchers Christina Congleton, Britta K. Hölzel and Sara W. Lazar, in their 2015 article, 'Mindfulness Can Literally Change Your Brain', speak about studying the participants of an eight-week mindfulness programme.

'We observed significant increases in the density of their grey matter. In the years since, other neuroscience laboratories from around the world have also investigated ways in which meditation, one key way to practise mindfulness, changes the brain. This year, a team of scientists from the University of British Columbia and the Chemnitz University of Technology were able to pool data from more than 20 studies to determine which areas of the brain are consistently affected. They identified at least eight different regions. Here we will focus on two that we believe to be of particular interest to business professionals.'

'The first is the anterior cingulate cortex (ACC), a structure located deep inside the forehead, behind the brain's frontal lobe. The ACC is associated with self-regulation, meaning the ability to purposefully direct attention and behaviour, suppress inappropriate knee-jerk responses, and switch strategies flexibly. People with damage to the ACC show impulsivity and unchecked aggression, and those with impaired connections between this and other brain regions perform poorly on tests of mental flexibility—they hold onto ineffective problem-solving strategies rather than adapting their behaviour. Meditators, on the other hand, demonstrate superior performance on tests of self-regulation, resisting distractions and making correct answers more often than non-meditators. They also show more activity in the ACC than non-meditators. In addition to self-regulation, the ACC is associated with learning from past experience to support optimal decision-making. Scientists point out that the ACC may be particularly important in the face of uncertain and fast-changing conditions.'

'The second brain region we want to highlight is the hippocampus, a region that showed increased amounts of grey matter in the brains of our 2011 mindfulness programme participants. This seahorse-shaped area is buried inside the temple on each side of the brain and is part of the limbic system, a set of inner structures associated with emotion and memory. It is covered in receptors for the stress hormone cortisol, and studies have shown that it can be damaged by chronic stress, contributing to a harmful spiral in the body. Indeed, people with stress-related disorders like depression and PTSD tend to have a smaller hippocampus. All of this points to the importance of this brain area in resilience—another key skill in the current high-demand business world.'

'These findings are just the beginning of the story. Neuroscientists have also shown that practising mindfulness affects brain areas related to perception, body awareness, pain tolerance, emotion regulation, introspection, complex thinking, and sense of self. While more research is needed to document these changes over time and to understand underlying mechanisms, the converging evidence is compelling.'

In a 2014 article on ScientificAmerican.com, Matthieu Ricard, Antoine Lutz and Richard J. Davidson speak of meditation having multitude of benefits for the mind and body. 'Researchers from several universities explored whether meditation might bring about structural changes in brain tissue. Using magnetic resonance imaging, they found that 20 experienced practitioners of one type of Buddhist meditation had a greater volume of brain tissue in the prefrontal cortex (Brodmann areas 9 and 10) and the insula than a control group did. These regions play a role in processing attention, sensory information and internal bodily sensations. Future long-term studies will be needed to confirm this finding.'[8]

Kabat-Zinn, a pioneer of scientific research on meditation, describes the benefits of meditation practice on the mind, brain and body. One of the main points he discusses is how meditation changes the brain structurally—neuroplasticity. 'Meditation can transform your life and be profoundly healing. And it does that by working on the entire organism—from your chromosomes to your cells to your brain. It affects all organ systems within the body. We're beginning to understand that, including the immune system and how the brain functions under stress and in difficult situations, how we regulate emotions and so forth.'

'The brain, being an organ of experience, is continually changing its shape. This is that kind of discovery of neuroplasticity. So how we decide to live our lives, and in the sense how we decide to keep our minds, changes not just our ideas and opinions and how caught we get in them, but also our relationship to thought. Then, when we look at the structure of the brain, not only is the brain functioning differently, but the actual structure of the brain, what some people call the real estate of the brain, is being recruited in the service of greater compassion, equanimity, clarity and wisdom. And you can see that different regions of the brain become thicker.'[9]

---

8   Source: https://www.law.upenn.edu/live/files/3918-mind-of-the-meditatorpdf
9   Source: http://www.meditationplex.com/meditation-benefits/jon-kabat-zinn-the-benefits-of-meditation/

CNN anchor and *60 Minutes* correspondent Anderson Cooper is one of the busiest journalists in the US. Like countless others, he's constantly working his mobile phone, probably more than most. Cooper attended a mindfulness retreat and learned about the benefits of meditation. He then met with Dr Judson Brewer, a psychiatrist and neuroscientist at the University of Massachusetts, and saw that the benefits of meditation are clearly visible via neurological measurements. Wearing a cap with 128 electrodes, which monitored his brain to show how meditation and mindfulness can alter its function, Cooper thought anxiety-provoking thoughts before beginning to meditate. Monitors showed his brain cells instantly reacting to the mindfulness technique. An initial spike in red lines corresponding to the brain cells triggering anxious thoughts settled into blue lines with meditation, indicating a decrease in the activity of those brain cells.

Dr Brewer believes everyone can learn to meditate and achieve the same mindfulness, as well as escape constant use of digital devices, which he believes are addictive.[10]

By now, your brain should have made the connection. But if not, and for those like me who are a bit slow, here are some pointers:

1. Creativity is an energy that allows you to do wonderful things.
2. All of us have this energy in abundance. We only need to allow it to shine forth.

---

[10] Sources: http://www.cbsnews.com/news/anderson-cooper-plugs-in-to-mindfulness/
http://www.huffingtonpost.in/entry/60-minutes-mindfulness_n_6324184

3. There are well-proven and established behaviour frameworks like design thinking that can already facilitate creative thinking.
4. Mindfulness is an ancient contemplative practice.
5. Mindfulness impacts many of the drivers of the behaviours recommended for enhancing creativity.
6. Mindfulness is an energy that opens up your aquifers of creativity.

Design is not how it looks. Design is how it works.

Steve Jobs

9. THE 10 LAWS OF CREATIVITY

As we get closer to embarking on our voyage of creative rediscovery, you must be marvelling at how the magical dance of creativity and creation plays out. To help you marvel a little more, here are my laws of creativity:

Law 1: The universe likes to create. It wants to manifest

Just look out your window. If you don't have a window, close your eyes and think of the universe. On this planet alone, millions and millions of life forms are constantly being created. There is a fascinating and endless dance of creation, manifestation and transformation. The little worm gets eaten by the fish that gets eaten by you and finally you are eaten by the worm. This may vary a bit depending on whether you eat fish or not. But you get the picture, right?

Law 2: All that is created takes some form

Music, books, paintings, products, services and even software are created when an idea takes shape and translates into form. Body, thought, emotion and energy are also forms.

Law 3: It takes doing for the form to get created

An idea that is not worked upon remains unformed. Unless you *do* something about it, it doesn't take form. Even the universe *does* something when it creates. Whether it is the Big Bang or water evaporating as steam, the laws of physics and chemistry show that the universe has *done* something.

Law 4: Most creations exist on a time-space continuum

Remember the theory of special relativity? Enough said.

Law 5: All creation comes from a state of no space and no time

Where do thoughts and ideas come from? An immensely vast state of no form and no doing, just being. Essentially, creation comes from a core of nothingness and being, but in doing, it pushes outwards towards form and complexity. Remember the Big Bang theory?

Maybe the Zen masters who spoke of the wisdom of non-resistance were on to something. For non-resistance comes from just being.

Law 6: A human being is a microcosm of the universe

Think about it.

Law 7: The laws of creativity that work in the universe also apply to humans

Believe in it.

Law 8: Humans create too

In fact, we create plenty! Just ask the folks in advertising. Humans can even create thoughts and emotions just sitting around with nothing to do. When humans *do* something, they create tangible stuff, and like the universe, that creativity too manifests *in* something.

Law 9: Like the universe, humans too create from a state of 'being'

Being, as you know, is formless, timeless and yet, simple. Remember the states all our creative heroes from history were in? Remember your own state when you are in the flow, when you lose sense of time and space and things seem to come together magically?

Law 10: The secret of unlimited creative energy lies in understanding, reconciling with and living these nine seemingly paradoxical laws

When you do that, you realise that human creation is unlimited in its potential and as vast as the creative power of the universe.

10. MANIFESTING YOUR MANTRA

Once you fully understand the 10 laws of creativity, you can manifest your own creative mantra—one that comes from the core of your being and takes into account who you are, where you are and what you are doing. A mantra that balances the formless within you and the form that exists in your life.

It is different for all of us. There is no correct mantra. The right mantra for you is the one that works for you. It evolves as you progress on your creative journey. Depending on where you stand, you will call to use different combinations and proportions of the practices shared in the following pages and slowly, your mantra will form.

Just do what feels right and let your instincts guide you. Once you know what works for you, it is not necessary that you remain there! Experimenting with other exercises and combinations may unlock something even more powerful. Milarepa, the Tibetan saint, once said, 'In the beginning nothing comes, in the middle nothing stays, in the end nothing goes.'

Daniel Goleman and Davidson, in their 2017 book on meditation and neuroscience, talk about how Buddhist monk Matthieu Ricard unpacks Milarepa's puzzle: 'At the start of contemplative practice, little or nothing seems to change in us. After continued practise, we notice some changes in our way of being, but they come and go. Finally, as the practice stabilises, the changes are constant and enduring, with no fluctuation. They are altered traits.'

So, as you work to manifest your creative genie, remember this beautiful interpretation could well apply to your practice. Happy manifesting!

PART B

Before you launch into this section of the book, make sure you've gotten yourself a creativity journal. It should be a special diary or a sketchbook with plenty of space to write, sketch, doodle, revisit to add notes, etc. Let it be a gift to yourself or a gift to you by someone who supports your creative journey. Understand the sanctity of this journal—it is going to witness your deepest and innermost thoughts and feelings as you nurture the miracles that will unfold across its pages.

Intent setting

There is a small but powerful ritual that needs to be done—once in the beginning and subsequently as many times as required while working through Part B.

Declare to the universe your intent to unlock your creative spirit.

The following lines are to be read aloud and then written on page one of your creativity journal.

> I will earnestly work through the exercises set out for me. In doing so, I believe that powerful creative forces will be set in motion within me and my creative genie will come alive.

The building blocks of mindfulness

Mindfulness can start with simple day-to-day exercises and extend to a whole lot of activities. In the following pages are instructions for some formal exercises as well as guidance on how to integrate the power of mindfulness into everyday aspects. These are meant to be signposts and as your practice evolves, you can integrate other pursuits into your practice of mindfulness.

Practise as many of these exercises as you are comfortable with. There is no right or wrong. The idea is to become familiar with them, weave them into your everyday life and build a solid platform of mindfulness energy.

'Oh wait! Active busy people like me don't have time to do all these things! I need to work on projects, solve problems, meet deadlines, deal with difficult people, and do a zillion other things. How am I to practise mindfulness?' If that is what you are thinking, then you are normal!

My response to you: Whatever, you are doing, keep your attention focused on it. Be alert and calm. You will handle everything that arises, in a better way. Mindfulness, as you will soon see, is not any different from focusing all your attention on whatever you are doing. So, when you are working on your project or solving problems or meeting deadlines or dealing with difficult people, a calm and clear mind, self-control and a kind heart are necessary for good results. I'm sure you will agree with that. So, mindfulness is actually a miracle that needs little or no extra time from you once you learn it!

Imagine a magician who cuts his body into many parts and scatters all the parts in different directions, and then utters a magic cry which then reassembles this body, bringing every part back into place. Mindfulness is exactly like that. It is the magic that can, in a flash, call back our scattered mind and focus it on the moment at hand.

In the following weeks, you will also build on many of these exercises in powerful ways. It is like a spiral track pushing upwards, and as you refine your creative mantra, your creative genie will slowly come alive.

So, how do you know you have done enough?

At some point, you will start to feel the energy of mindfulness in your life. The energy of consciousness. You will feel more present and alive. For one of my students Jay, it happened on Day Three and for another, Sara, it took a bit longer. But most people feel a perceptible shift when it happens. Irrespective of who you're like, do these exercises for at least six days (the boot camp), and then start Week 1 of your course in creativity.

Just remember not to try too hard! Stay intense, not tense, and relaxed but not lax. Above all, have fun!

Note: Finding a mindfulness buddy can be a fun and powerful way to engage in these practices. It could be someone who is going on this journey with you, or someone supportive who will read out some of the exercise instructions to you if you feel the need. Try it!

11. THE SIX-DAY BOOT CAMP

In the boot camp, we introduce to you six formal and several informal exercises. The former are, in a sense, the building blocks of your mindfulness practice, while the latter are opportunities to integrate mindfulness into daily life. Formal practices need dedicated effort for a certain period of time, but the informal ones are things you already do—we only alter the way you do them. In fact, you could get really creative and keep increasing the number of informal exercises as you go along, until one day life itself becomes a series of informal mindfulness practices.

> *The real meditation is how you live your life.*
>
> Jon Kabat-Zinn

Each day, introduce yourself to one formal practice and a few informal ones. You may want to continue practising the techniques learnt on the previous days as you progress (very, very highly encouraged), in addition to learning new exercises for that day.

Day 1

The first of these formal practices is a body scan meditation. As simple as it may sound, this is an important foundation for most other mindfulness practices. Why? Well, for one, it creates a relaxed mind that facilitates better focus and awareness. This, in turn, sets you up for other practices, which require a greater deal of concentration. Secondly, the monkey mind loves rushing from one thing to another. Asking it to focus on one object or your breath straightaway would be difficult. By giving it body part after body part to focus on, you feed it variety, and yet keep it in one place.

I like the second explanation more. It's more fun!

Formal Practice 1: Body Scan

TIME

30 to 40 minutes

CAUTION

Have you gone through abuse or trauma? If yes, please do this exercise with a trained professional. Otherwise, if you notice severe mental or physical discomfort or pain, discontinue and check in with a trained mindfulness teacher.

STEPS

To begin, choose a sitting or lying down position, whatever is comfortable for you, in a quiet space. If you are sitting, choose a sturdy, straight-back chair. Your feet should touch the ground when you sit in the chair. If you are lying down, roll out a mat and make sure there is enough space around your body.

Sit with your back straight and soles of the feet planted into the ground, with the knees positioned above the ankles. Rest your palms on your knees. Use a cushion if you have any back-related issues. Alternately, lie on your back in a comfortable position with your eyes closed.

Notice the points of the body in contact with the floor or the chair. Allow these points to relax and sense gravity pulling them downwards. If you are sitting, feel the palms relaxing and getting heavier on your knees.

Take a moment to observe the whole body from top to bottom, with your mind focused completely on the body.

Now, take your awareness to your breathing. Notice as you breathe in and breathe out. Pay attention to the rise and fall of the chest/belly. Do this 10 times. It is likely that your mind will wander to other things (it's a monkey, I know). Worry not, just be aware of the distraction and bring your focus back to the breathing every time this happens.

Slowly shift your awareness to the toes of the right foot. Be curious and keenly notice all the sensations you feel in them, be it heat or cold, tingling or tightness or anything else. It's OK if there is no sensation. If the toes are tense, allow them to soften with every breath out. Also, be aware of any emotions or thoughts if they arise without judging them. Keep your attention on the toes for several breaths, until you feel you have attended to them fully.

Now direct your attention to the top of the right foot. Apply the same process as you did with the toes.

In this way, go through the ankle, calf, shin, knee, thigh and groin of the right leg.

Follow up with a similar survey of the left foot and leg. Move on to the belly, chest, followed by the buttocks, and lower, middle and upper back.

Continue to the right arm, beginning with the fingers and moving on to the palms, the back of the hand, wrist, forearm, elbow, upper arm and shoulder. Repeat with the left arm.

Move on to the front and back of the neck, the chin, mouth, cheeks, nose and eyes, spending sufficient time on each part. Proceed to the forehead, ears, the back of the head and finally, the top of the head.

Make sure you feel each region of the body as deeply and precisely as you can. Practise accepting what you discover about each part. At any point, if you notice that the mind has wandered, gently bring it back to focus.

Finally, become aware of the whole body and rest for a few minutes in this expansive awareness.

Now take your awareness to your breathing. Simply observe the movement of breath in and out of the body. Keep the mind focused on your breathing and bring it back lest it wanders. Do this 20 times or until you feel you own the breath or are in complete control of breathing without getting distracted.

Gently shift your focus back to your body. Attend to the fingers and toes, move them very slowly. Sense the entire body coming out of the experience.

Open your eyes when you feel ready to.

Note: It is generally advised to spend 30 to 40 minutes to complete the body scan. However, if you wish to do a shorter body scan, spend less time on each region, and/or focus on both feet, legs and arms together as you move through them. You can also practise the body scan in the opposite direction, moving from your head to your toes.

For informal exercises for Day 1, pick any two from pages 81 to 85.

Osho explains the four steps of relaxation in meditation—body, mind, heart and being.

'Remember as many times as possible to look into the body, whether you are carrying some tension in the body somewhere—at the neck, in the head, in the legs. Relax it consciously. Just go to that part of the body and persuade that part, say to it lovingly, "Relax!"

And you will be surprised to know that if you approach any part of your body, it listens, it follows you—it is your body! With closed eyes, go inside the body from the toe to the head, searching for any place where there is tension. And then talk to that part as you talk to a friend; let there be a dialogue between you and your body. Tell it to relax, and tell it, "There is nothing to fear. Don't be afraid. I am here to take care—you can relax." Slowly, slowly, you will learn the knack of it. Then, the body becomes relaxed.

Then, take another step, a little deeper; tell the mind to relax. And if the body listens, mind also listens, but you cannot start with the mind—you have to start from the beginning. You cannot start from the middle. Many people start with the mind and they fail; they fail because they start from the wrong place. Everything should be done in the right order.

If you become capable of relaxing the body voluntarily, then you will be able to help your mind relax voluntarily. Mind is a more complex phenomenon. Once you have become confident that the body listens to you, you will have a new trust in yourself. Now even the mind can listen to you. It will take a little longer with the mind, but it happens.

When the mind is relaxed, then start relaxing your heart, the world of your feelings, emotions—which is even more complex, more subtle. But now you will be moving with trust, with great trust in yourself. Now you will know it is possible. If it is possible with the body and possible with the mind, it is possible with the heart, too. And then only when you have gone through these three steps can you take the fourth. Now you can go to the innermost core of your being, which is beyond body, mind, heart—the very centre of your existence. And you will be able to relax it too.

And that relaxation certainly brings the greatest joy possible, the ultimate in ecstasy, acceptance. You will be full of bliss and rejoicing. Your life will have the quality of dance to it.'

The Dhammapada: The Way of the Buddha Vol. 1, Chapter 8

Day 2

Formal Practice 2: Writing Meditation

Writing meditation is a powerful mindfulness tool that's particularly useful for beginners who find it difficult to do body scan and methods like seated or breath awareness meditation. Writing gives your mind something to focus on, so there are fewer chances of it wandering, thus bringing you into the present moment.

TIME
10 to 15 minutes

STEPS
To get started, choose a space where you can write comfortably and without disturbance. Keep a timer, your creativity journal and a pen ready.

Begin by staying seated in silence with your eyes closed. Feel the body settling down and becoming still. Become aware of the space and sounds around you. Shift attention to your breathing—simply observe it without changing its pace. Start counting your breaths as you inhale and exhale. It is only natural that various thoughts will arise in the mind. When that happens, gently refocus your attention on your breathing without beating yourself up. Take 30 conscious breaths.

Your mind will now be calmer than before. Prepare by telling yourself you will be open to the experience without judging. Set the timer for 10 minutes.

Start with the prompt words, 'in this moment', and write without pausing to think. Write continuously, pouring out whatever comes to mind. It does not matter what it is, neither does it have to be grammatically correct. All you are doing is capturing the thoughts skimming the surface of your mind on paper. Write at a speed comfortable for you, and if you get stuck, prompt yourself with 'in this moment'. Remember, there are no judgements. So, if you find your mind wandering to make sense of what you are writing, gently coax it back to the act of writing. If you have nothing to write, write 'I have nothing to write', but keep going until the timer goes off.

Put the pen down, close your eyes and take three deep breaths. Observe how you feel after this free-flowing writing exercise.

Now, slowly read aloud (or whisper) what you've written. The idea is to concentrate fully on every word. At the same time, observe any emotions that arise at any point. Be open to them.

After reading, briefly jot down anything you want. If you want to probe or further understand anything you've written, make a note or underline it. You may use this as a prompt for the next writing session. If you are in the flow in the present moment, you could write for another 10 to 15 minutes using this prompt—it will help you delve deeper and access thoughts that haven't been obvious to you. Ensure that you follow the same steps as explained for the additional practice.

Doing this regularly will lead to phenomenal spontaneity in your writing. It will also help vastly in acceptance of the self. In time, you'll be able to understand yourself better and fuel your writing from a grounded presence. And the best part is that this practice can be done anywhere, anytime.

Day 3

Formal Practice 3: Walking Meditation

Think of this as mindfulness in motion. As a formal practice, walking meditation is especially helpful when the mind is restless, the body stiff and one is sleepy. It can also be an informal practice that you can incorporate into your daily walkabout whenever you feel the need to dial into a more mindful state.

TIME
15 to 20 minutes

STEPS
Choose a quiet space with a fairly long path of about 30 feet. A grass or sand patch will also do. It's important that you are undisturbed on this path, hence, to start, choose an isolated one (so you don't get distracted and start wondering what anyone watching you may think when they see you in practice).

Stand barefoot at the beginning of your path. Close your eyes and adjust your posture, keeping your spine straight. Press the soles of your feet into the ground. Feel a deep connection with the earth. This is the grounding process.

Gently move your awareness up your body, becoming more mindful of each part until you reach the top of the head. Become aware of the body as a whole. Sense the air around you, wherever it touches your skin. Listen to the sounds. Notice your breath at the nostrils, observing the flow of air and the sensations as you breathe in and out.

Once you have settled into the experience of standing, slowly open your eyes and look at the ground a few feet ahead of you. Observe this space with curiosity, taking in all its visual aspects—colour, form and texture.

Prepare to start walking. Shift your weight to one foot and slowly lift the other foot—it's almost as if you're walking for the first time. As you do, be completely aware of the sensations in the entire leg. Observe what happens at the root of the thighs, the knees, calves and shins. Then, gently place the foot on the ground, again tuning into the sensations as the sole touches the earth. Now lift the other foot and repeat the process. Do this at a pace that helps you to maintain balance and continue walking slowly to the end of the path.

Pause for a few moments and repeat the grounding process. Enjoy the stillness, reconnect with the earth, air and the sounds around you.

Once you are recentred, turn around slowly and walk back to the beginning of the path following the same steps as before.

Continue this walking meditation for about 20 minutes.

Informally, you can integrate walking meditation practice into your daily walkabout. You may choose to increase your pace as it may not be possible to maintain such a slow pace. However, attend to the sensations as much as you can. It will help develop concentration and move you to a mindful state.

Day 4

Formal Practice 4: Eating Meditation

How would you like to eat less and feel thoroughly satisfied? Sounds contradictory, huh? But eating meditation helps you become mindful and keeps your weight in check at the same time. Talk about having the cake and eating it too!

TIME
5 to 10 minutes (or as long as you want)

STEPS
This practice is also called raisin meditation because—you guessed right—it's done with a raisin. So, keep a few raisins handy before you start.

Sit comfortably in a chair, straighten your spine and firmly plant your feet on the ground. Keep a raisin on your palm and rest the palms on your lap. Close your eyes.

Feel your body settling into a state of calm. Gently shift your awareness to your breathing. Observe its natural flow for a few seconds, then take three deep breaths feeling completely present in the moment. Open your eyes and look down at your palms.

Shift your focus to the raisin. Pick it up using your thumb and index finger and bring it to eye level. Look at the raisin intently. What is the form? What colour is it? Do you notice the ridges on its surface? How deep are they? Does the raisin have a top and a bottom? Is it shiny or dull? Gently squeeze the raisin and explore its texture. Do you feel it against your skin? Is it hard, soft or squishy, or something in-between? Stay completely focused on exploring these qualities.

Now close your eyes and do not open them until the end of the exercise. Roll the raisin close to your ear between your thumb and forefinger using moderate pressure. Do you hear faint sounds? Do they remind you of anything?

Bring the raisin beneath your nostrils and smell it. Is the scent inviting or unpleasant? Or, is it neither? Does the smell incite any thoughts or memories?

Slowly move the raisin to the mouth and touch it to the lips. Keep your mouth closed and let the raisin stay there for a while. Observe the sensation as soon as it touches the lips. Can you feel the texture? Does it cause any changes inside the mouth?

Then, place the raisin on your tongue. Do not bite into it yet, just let it lie on your tongue for a few seconds. Can you taste anything? Roll it around your mouth. Be aware of the reactions inside the mouth.

Now, gently bite into the raisin. What is the first thing that hits you as the raisin is sliced through? Notice if there is salivation and the extent of salivation. Does the first taste that hits you bring any images to mind?

Now very, very slowly start chewing with complete awareness as you continue to observe the changes in texture, form and taste. Visualise the backstory of the raisin. Imagine it as a grape on the vine soaking up the sun, water and fresh air. Can you taste any of the elements that nurtured it?

Once you are done chewing, gently swallow the raisin and follow the movement of the raisin into your stomach. Observe the aftertaste in your mouth. Stay still for a few seconds, experiencing having eaten a raisin with all your senses.

If you wish to, continue the exercise with another raisin. Start the process from the beginning. If you feel you're done with the experience, slowly open your eyes.

This is a fairly elaborate exercise in eating and possibly how many of our ancestors ate, respecting the food they grew with their own hands and feeling grateful to Mother Nature for every bite. We've moved as far away from that as we can with our TV dinners, eating while driving or chatting on the phone, and sometimes just eating to fill our tummies within a limited time before rushing off to the next meeting. No wonder we look and feel this way. We are what we eat. And I dare say we are how we eat too!

Certainly, it's impractical to eat every meal like this. Your friends and family might think you've become a bit weird after reading this book. But try eating one meal a day like this. If that's not possible, how about having one bite or one sip with all your senses, slowly, mindfully, at every meal? That is definitely doable. Then watch how both your diet and you change.

Day 5

Formal Practice 5: Getting to Ness

This is a mindfulness exercise we'll repeat frequently right through the journey.

TIME
5 to 10 minutes (or as long as you want)

STEPS
Sit comfortably in a chair at a table or with your legs crossed on the floor. Keep your back straight and spine erect. Place a cushion under you or to support your back if you need—make sure you are relaxed.

Now close your eyes and take a deep breath, as deeply as you can. Feel the breath going all the way in and filling up your belly. Let your lungs and rib cage expand as you feel it fill you up all the way to your shoulders. Hold it for a moment and then gently exhale, starting with your belly to your shoulders. Repeat two more times before you return to normal breathing.

Keeping your eyes closed, focus on the sensation of the breath. Feel it in your nostrils. Is it warm? Is it cold? What do you feel in your body as you focus on your breathing? If there is a gentle tingling in the nose or face, it's perfectly fine. Visualise your breath as a stream, going in and out, with a beginning and an end. As you breathe in, the beginning of the stream goes all the way down into your body to the deepest place you can feel. At this point, the end of the stream has disappeared into your nostrils. As you breathe out, the end of the stream emerges, coming out all the way until its head is at your nostrils again. Can you visualise it in a dazzling white light? Repeat this process for as long as you want, with at least four to five repetitions.

Now, do you realise there is a split-second gap between your inhalation and exhalation? Likewise, there's a mini pause after you exhale and before you inhale. As you keep breathing, focus on this gap. See how long it is. Don't force it but merely become very aware of it. Notice that the body has relaxed and the mind has quietened.

If you have done this in pin-drop silence with absolutely no disturbance, you might feel your presence in a new and beautiful way that will bring a smile to your face. Whenever you are ready, gently open your eyes.

Imagine a huge towering wall—one with no apparent way to climb, but only a thin thread hanging over the top and coming down on both the sides. A smart person would probably first tie a slightly thicker and stronger string to it and then pull on the other side to loop the string over the wall. Then, they could tie a rope to the string and pull the rope over before using the rope to scale the wall. Similarly, our breath is like that fragile thread. But, once we learn how to use it, it can allow us to do amazing things. It is the bridge between body and mind. The single tool that is with us from the moment we are born and everywhere we go, till the moment we die!

La Dolce Far Niente

Elizabeth Gilbert, in her memoir *Eat, Pray, Love: One Woman's Search for Everything Across Italy, India and Indonesia* popularised the concept of *la dolce far niente*, which means pleasant relaxation in carefree idleness. But those who're steeped in a busy life might view this sweet idleness as sheer laziness.

Italians are famous for wandering off mid-day for a siesta or a glass of wine at a nearby café. They discovered the power of doing nothing and fiercely guard the ritual. Those of us who just *do* all the time tend to dream of quiet peaceful locales to escape to as soon as time permits, but it's much simpler than that. Let's learn from the Italians who weave *la dolce far niente* into their everyday to nurture a state of mind where creativity brews willingly and happily. Their designs are proof.

> Clinical psychologist Colleen Long in her article, 'The Art of Doing Nothing', says,
> 'That kind of relaxation exists within each of us and is ours for the taking if we're willing to put in the effort.'

Day 6

Formal Practice 6: Breath Awareness Meditation

A deeper version of the earlier exercise, there is absolutely no substitute for this. It's the foundation attention-training exercise required for all other techniques, and as discussed earlier, breath awareness meditation is the equivalent of basic physical fitness required for all sport. In fact, this is how we should be breathing all the time. But we forget and lose our minds and bodies (quite literally) to shallow breaths that deprive our cells of energy and the mind of calm. Let's restore them, shall we?

TIME
Start with 15 minutes in the beginning, but as you deepen your practice, extend this to a minimum 30 minutes

STEPS
You can choose to do this either on a chair or sitting in a comfortable position on the floor. If you are using a chair, ensure you can sit with your spine straight and feet touching the floor. On the floor, sit cross-legged with the spine straight. In both the cases, feel free to take back support if

you need, especially if you have back-related issues. If you are using a meditation cushion sitting on the floor, make sure your knees touch the floor and there's a stable triangle formed by the knees and buttocks.

Rest your palms on your knees and close your eyes. Become aware of the parts of the body touching the floor or the chair. Sense them relaxing. Ensure there is no tension in the shoulder and neck area. If you feel any, gently rotate the shoulders backward and forward. Move your head from side to side, backward and forward to release tightness, then return to the original position and remain absolutely still as far as possible.

To ensure that the spine is erect and long, imagine a string attached to the top of your head pulling you upwards. Maintain this straight spine throughout the exercise.

Once you are settled and comfortable, shift awareness to your breathing. Notice the normal breathing pattern. Become aware of your sensations as you breathe in and out. Notice the passage of air. Are there any other places in the body where you sense changes? It is likely that your mind will wander many times during this exercise. Every time that happens, gently bring it back to focus on your breath and start from the beginning.

Slowly, try to deepen your breathing without excessive effort. Counting while exhaling could help. As your skill builds, you'll be able to increase the number of counts before a thought crosses your mind. Your regular breathing pattern will also deepen.

Do this for 15 to 30 minutes until you feel completely grounded. Whenever you are ready to end the session, gently revert attention to the body, and as you return to normal breathing, become aware of the body as a whole. When done, gently open your eyes.

> In the Sutras, the Buddha often teaches the secret of concentration using one's breath. The sutra which speaks about the use of breath to maintain mindfulness is the Anapanasati Sutra. Anapana means breath and sati as you will recall, is memory or mindfulness. So, the Anapanasati Sutra is the sutra on using one's breath to maintain mindfulness. It is the 118th sutra in the Mahayana Nikaya collection of sutras and it teaches 16 methods of using one's breath.

Informal Practices

Brushing teeth: You are probably wondering how such a mundane, routine activity can be mindful. Well, that's exactly why it is! Because we do it every day, we are in autopilot mode when doing things like brushing our teeth, shaving or having a shower. Why does it have to be an activity you have to get out of the way? Flip your thinking. Use it as an opportunity to foster mindfulness.

When starting to brush, become aware of what you can see, hear, feel and taste. Notice the colour of the toothpaste, its form on the brush as you squeeze it out and the smell. Slow your movements. Sense the initial taste and texture as the brush touches the teeth. Be mindful of your movements as you brush from side to side, and up and down. Close your eyes if you want. Notice the sensations on the teeth and gums. Listen to the sounds as you brush. Enjoy the cleansing feeling as you rinse your mouth. In short, brush as if you are brushing for the first time. Close your eyes when you're done and savour the mindful experience of having brushed with all your attention.

Taking a shower: This routine activity can also be slowed down and experienced with a lot more awareness.

Apart from bringing you into the present moment by concentrating on every movement, scent, touch and sound, it can also be a mind-cleansing activity.

When you shower, imagine washing away your stress. Sense the water on your skin. As you soap, visualise anger, fear, regret, hatred and other negative emotions getting cleansed. Feel them flowing off you and down the drain.

Deep listening: Yes, conversation can also be an exercise in mindfulness, and this one is relevant considering what poor listeners we have become. We listen with the intent of replying; before someone even completes their sentence, we are crafting our responses because we are eager to offer an opinion or retaliate. Instead, try slowing down and giving the other person the complete gift of your attention. Be present. All you hear is the other person talking, word by word, without any other thoughts, without framing any responses. After the person has finished speaking, try to recall what he or she said before you respond.

Commuting or driving: This is an area we can really work on to bring ourselves into the present. As drivers, this can be a challenging task. Before starting the car, take a minute or two to tune into your breathing like you did in breath awareness meditation. Decide to give your complete attention to driving until you reach your destination.

Starting from turning the key in the ignition, be aware of your every move. When the mind wanders, consciously bring it back to the road, and your hands and feet on the controls. Keep your ears open to sounds around you. On tough stretches like bad roads, poor traffic or other drivers making things difficult for you, observe how your mind reacts. Are you getting disturbed or are you able to remain calm? Tell yourself you are sharing the road with others and being kind and empathetic is the best thing to do. Drive at moderate speeds without competing, and enjoy it.

For commuters it's pretty much the same principle of bringing attention to the details of the journey. The only difference is that you are not in control. Observe the sights and sounds around you, notice the driver and your co-passengers. Slow down your breathing while you are at it. Inhale and exhale deeply as you feel yourself completely present and watch the world around you.

Washing the dishes: This is a tedious chore, but it can become pleasurable with a change in perspective. What's more, it's going to relax you. Approach it not with the intent of getting it done, rather, wash the dishes with the intent of washing them. Makes no sense? Read on!

Consider each plate or bowl as an object of contemplation. Put all your attention into rinsing, soaping and washing. Follow your breath to keep your attention from diverting. Don't hurry. This is a meditative activity. Clean the dishes one by one, feel your stress wash away with the food particles. Once you put the last dish away, close your eyes and experience the satisfaction of having given the activity your full attention.

Chores: Whatever work you do at home, such as cleaning or arranging your knick-knacks, can easily become an opportunity for mindfulness.

If you have a series of things to do, plan and decide the order of your tasks. Before you begin, close your eyes, take a few deep breaths and centre yourself. Then apply yourself completely to the task. Slow down considerably and be completely immersed without thinking of what next or anything else. Remember, it's not about finishing the job but enjoying it.

For example, if you are dusting, pay close attention to the objects you're touching and moving out of the way. Move them one by one, looking at each object with curiosity. As you clear the dust with a cloth or duster, be attentive of every inch of space you clean, reaching into every nook and cranny. As you do this, imagine your soul getting cleansed too. Maintain the same attitude as you clean the objects as well and mindfully place them back where they were.

In the end, pause and review your work. Close your eyes and be thankful for all that you own and the place you live.

Move on to the next task and apply the same mindful attention to it. You will enjoy the activity, and with practise, you might even look forward to household chores because they give you an opportunity to tune into your mindful frequency.

Listening to music: Listening to music is usually pleasurable, an activity most of us end up doing mindfully quite often. Yes, pat yourself on the back. You are not a novice at mindfulness at all! It's just that we've forgotten to be mindful in other aspects of life. Try it with a favourite track every day.

Ready the music in a space of your choice, preferably one that's quiet. If there are chances of disturbance, keep earphones handy. Before you play the track, sit with your eyes closed and settle in with the intention of giving the music your full attention. Take a few breaths to centre yourself. Now, with complete awareness, press the play button, mindful of the movement of your hand and fingers. Close your eyes and pay more attention than you usually would to every note and word, and allow the music to wash over you. Observe how your mind reacts to the music. Notice any emotions that may arise without judging them. Continue to focus with the same attention until the track is over. Stay with the experience. Be thankful for your hearing. Observe how you feel. Then, slowly open your eyes.

12. WEEK 1: DEALING WITH OUR FEAR OF EVALUATION

If you know the enemy and you know yourself, you need not fear the result of a hundred battles. If you know yourself but not the enemy, for every victory gained you will also suffer a defeat. If you know neither the enemy nor yourself, you will succumb in every battle.

Sun Tzu

Inspired by the ancient Chinese philosopher Sun Tzu, in Week 1, we will start a dialogue with the chief of the creativity goblins, Mr Evaluation.

He finds his way into our lives when we are still young. Remember the picture of the sun you painted as a child? It was an irregular yellow circle with crooked lines sticking out of it, and your teacher and parents said it was very good. Well, Mr Evaluation, Chief Creativity Goblin, was born then.

As you kept quiet in school because quiet was good and didn't voice your opinion because arguing was bad, Mr Evaluation started growing bigger and stronger. You started gravitating towards things that led to good evaluations and avoided or hid those that led to bad evaluations. Growing up, you even learnt to act, think and feel as if things were good or bad in themselves. So, drunkards became bad and priests became good. Dreaming became bad and efficiency became good. As long as you behaved in accordance with these definitions, life was good and the Chief Creativity Goblin had you firmly in his grasp.

There's only one small problem.

A person who never made a mistake, never tried anything new.

Albert Einstein

I'm not advocating that you ignore the danger of making a mistake and cross a busy road when the walk sign is red. All I'm doing is inviting you to see the paradox.

Let me share a personal story. I've had little formal schooling. Until I was 13, I was home-schooled by my writer-teacher parents, so as a result, I don't have some of the more established behaviour patterns we see around us today. Looking back armed with knowledge of neuroscience, I wonder what kind of neurological connections were established in my childhood. For example, the need to be the first one with an answer isn't in me. I'm often happy to just walk around with a problem or ponder a question from multiple perspectives without a sense of urgency. I've found joy in exploring different subjects, even though I sometimes failed the exam.

I did my graduate studies first in science, then the arts—an uncommon combination in an age where you are expected to know your professional calling by the age of three or be deemed a failure. I've worked in the corporate world as a manager, consultant and designer, and been an entrepreneur with a couple of successful start-ups, and more than a few failed ones. In hindsight, I feel that a large part of my journey had to do with not fearing mistakes and never desiring to walk the beaten path. At IDEO, a client once said, 'It shows', when I shared an audacious idea for his company and, in another context, told him I was not formally schooled. I never summoned the courage to ask him exactly what he meant.

We are all abundantly creative, but as we grow up, our fear of evaluation, and the need to conform and enjoy the praise that comes with it become barriers to our creativity. Many times, we need to be non-conformist and reject the fear of evaluation to create something new.

Why did people praise your first drawing of the sun? Because you were a complete beginner. But at six or seven years, if you drew the sun in the same way, you would have been judged. 'Look at that kid. His/her drawing is so much better' is what you would have heard. Slowly, you would have stopped drawing. Do you know why most adults draw like kids? The skill is killed at some point during childhood by the fear of evaluation. Those who overcome the fear become artists.

So, make the most of inexperience and remain a beginner in your mind, open to anything. Don't *know* how things *should* be done. If you don't get stuck with what is *right*, nothing in particular would be *wrong*. You can grow older without growing up.

The world needs creativity and originality more than ever. Ironically, it's within us, but we go about seeking it elsewhere and in others. So, stop evaluating yourself constantly against the perfect son or daughter or the perfect husband or wife or the perfect employee. Remember, their drawings of the sun were no different from yours.

If we can learn to live mindfully, we can understand how evaluation works in us. We can see that it's necessary only in certain situations. We can learn not to be held hostage by it.

At IDEO, you see an element of play everywhere and little or no fear of evaluation. When Steve Jobs asked David Kelly to come up with a revolutionary new design for the mouse, he hadn't bargained for what he got. David and his team of grown-ups had fun playing around with scraps and toys, and presented Jobs the ball of a deodorant roll attached to an optoelectronic system. Being a visionary, Jobs recognised the genius of the mishmash in front of him, and the mouse you use today was born.

A large part of the fear of being evaluated comes from thinking that one may not know the right answer. But creativity comes from not knowing; it comes from messing around, not knowing what one is doing. Seeking without the need to find.

Nobel laureate Subrahmanyan Chandrasekhar's work was on black holes, and he taught astrophysics at the University of Chicago. Initially, only two students—Tsung-Dao Lee and Chen-Ning Yang—signed up for his course. The perfect lecturers pride themselves on conducting popular classes with high attendance and so, this became a joke among Chandrasekhar's colleagues. People expected him to cancel the class, especially because he had to commute nearly 130 kilometres to the observatory where he was to take it. But Chandrasekhar was not perturbed by their evaluation. He and his students loved what they did—they had fun exploring new ideas and didn't care that they were mocked for being the smallest class in the history of university education.

In 1957, Lee and Yang won the Nobel Prize in Physics, while Chandrasekhar received the coveted award in 1983.

The smallest class had become the most successful university class, where everyone involved had won a Nobel!

So, stay young, remain a beginner, stay playful and put evaluation in its right place. Research says joking around within limits is good. Playfulness opens people up to new possibilities, makes them less sensitive to poor evaluations (because they are just kidding) and puts them in a relaxed state where creative energies can flow freely.

Development psychologist Howard Gardner has studied many people who shaped the last century through their creative genius. He found that although many of them reached the limits of knowledge in their chosen fields, they retained a childlike freshness in their approach. Hence, Einstein, although an expert physicist by the age of 20, often wondered what it would be like to travel in a beam of light.

With that, let's kick off this week!

Renew your intent for the week by repeating your declaration to the universe that's provided in the beginning of Part B.

Day 1

Exercise 1: Body Scan

Exercise 2: Letting Go of Situations

This exercise is important in that it paves the way for the exercises that follow on other days, so please do full justice to it.

You are going to get to know the enemy and yourself!

TIME
10 to 15 minutes (or as long as you want)

STEPS
1. Choose an object from everyday life. It could be a pebble, a piece of paper you can crumple, a cloth or even a balloon—something you are prepared to let go.
2. Sit comfortably in a chair with your back straight. Place your hands on your knees with palms facing upwards and hold the chosen object in one hand. Keep your head straight and close your eyes.
3. Recall the memory of an incident when evaluation did not work favourably for you, an instance when you strongly felt you were assessed unfairly. It could be from any period and any area of your life. It should be an incident that shook your confidence in your creative ability—perhaps a childhood drawing your teacher criticised and your classmates laughed, or a solution to a problem your boss shot down. Let it be something that evokes a reasonably strong (but not violent) emotion and a memory you have carried in life. Relive it and the emotion as intensely as you can, holding the object in your hands, noticing the points in your body where the emotions are manifesting. Finally, pour it all into the object. When you are ready to move on, it should feel as if the object contains everything associated with that incident.
4. Continue sitting in the same position, keeping your back straight. Make sure you are comfortable and if that means adjusting a cushion under you or to support your back, that's fine. With your eyes closed, take a deep breath, as deeply as you can. Feel it going all the way in and filling up your belly. Let your lungs and rib cage expand as you feel the breath fill you all the way to your shoulders. Hold it for a moment and then gently exhale, starting from your belly to your shoulders. Repeat a few times before you return to normal breathing.

5. Now focus on the sensation of the breath. Feel it in your nostrils. What do you feel in your body as you focus on the breath? Visualise your breath as a stream, going in and out, with a beginning and an end. As you breathe in, the beginning of the stream goes all the way down into your body to the deepest place you can feel. At this point, the end of the stream has disappeared into your nostrils. As you breathe out, the end of the stream emerges, coming out all the way until its head is at your nostrils again. Repeat this process for as long as you want, with at least four to five repetitions. The body has relaxed. The mind has also quietened.

6. Whenever you are ready, recall the memory again. Recall the emotion it comes with and your belief that it blocks your creativity. Remember, everything is now contained in the object you have injected the memory into. It is possible that you feel a lot more dispassionate about the incident as well as the object you are holding. That is perfectly fine. The negative beliefs that were created in the situation have all now been transferred to the object. When you are ready, let the object go. Just drop it softly or open your hands and let it fall out. When you are ready, gently open your eyes.

Congratulations! You just fired Mr Evaluation from your life!

Observe what you are experiencing. Continue breathing mindfully, becoming aware of the sensation of the breath until you feel completely calm. You may feel mild elation as you feel liberated from the memory that has troubled you for so long. Accept it without getting drawn into a celebration, at least, not a big one. For as you refocus on your breath, this feeling too will pass.

Do this exercise as many times as you wish and whenever you feel the need to let go of something you feel holds your creative energy back.

Exercise 3: Writing Meditation

In your creativity journal, record what you felt during the body scan and the exercise of letting go.

TIME
10 minutes of free flow writing

STEPS
1. Choose a space where you can write comfortably and without disturbance. Keep a timer, your creativity journal and pen ready.
2. To begin, stay seated in silence with your eyes closed. Feel the body settling down and becoming still. Become aware of the space and sounds around you. Shift attention to your breathing. Observe it without changing the pace. Start counting your breaths as you notice your inhales and exhales. Various thoughts will arise in the mind. If that happens, take 30 conscious breaths. You mind will be calmer than before. Tell yourself that you'll remain open to the experience without judging. Set the timer for 10 minutes.
3. Begin by writing the prompt words 'When I let go, I...' and write whatever comes to mind without pausing to think. Write continuously, pouring out everything. It does not matter what it is, neither does it have to be grammatically correct. All you are doing is capturing the thoughts skimming the surface of the mind on paper. Do not stop writing. Write at a pace comfortable for you. If you get stuck, use the prompt 'When I let go, I...' again and let more thoughts flow. Remember, there is no judgement. If you find your mind wandering to make sense of what you are writing, gently coax it back to your breathing and the act of writing. Keep doing this until the timer goes off.

4. Pause, put the pen down and close your eyes to take three deep breaths. Observe how you feel after free flow writing.

Celebrating mistakes and failures the wabi-sabi way

Takeno Jōō, one of Japan's earliest tea masters, wrote, 'If a friend visits you, make him tea, warmly wish him welcome with hospitality, set up some flowers and make him feel comfortable.' This is embodied in the common Japanese phrase *shaza kissa,* which translates to, 'Well, sit down and have some tea.'

In this age-old Japanese tradition of tea drinking lies one of the most beautiful and elegant ways of celebrating life, including creation and its mistakes. In this extremely mindful ritual of making the tea, pouring it gracefully and sharing a meaningful conversation with a visitor, friend or loved one resides a deep appreciation of how things are. The tea ritual, in fact, cultivates a mindset. One is taught to handle every utensil, right from the bamboo water scoop to the tea bowl as if it were extremely precious, like a rare antique. In doing so, do you hide or gloss over the shades of grey that years of usage have brought to the scoop or try to hide the slight crack that has developed in the tea bowl? No. In fact, much to the contrary, you celebrate these imperfections and treat the object with respect.

From this tradition comes the concept of wabi-sabi. In its barest essence, it is the Japanese art of finding beauty in imperfection, accepting the natural cycle of growth, decay and death and seeing profundity in it. Wabi-sabi is about celebrating cracks and crevices, frayed edges, rusted spots, asymmetry, exposed brick and decaying leaves. Wabi-sabi is about grey hair, wrinkles, crow's feet, a crooked tooth and a shuffle.

What qualify are things that you admire and love to use, like the old can opener that still works well. Things that are alive with the spirit of their makers, things that resonate the warmth of their makers' hands and hearts. The rocking chair your grandfather made, your five-year-old's lumpy pottery, a sweater you knitted yourself, perhaps. Pieces of your own history: Sepia-toned ancestral photos, baby clothes, the dog-eared Enid Blyton books you read over and over again as a kid.

Wabi-sabi is not to be found in a shiny iPhone or a new car. It's not in glass-and-steel skyscrapers, glitzy sales pitches or Excel spreadsheets! It is an aesthetic of simplicity hidden right in front of us that reveals itself through the daily work of living.

Wabi stems from the root word *wa*, which refers to harmony, peace, tranquillity, and balance. Wabi had the original meaning of sad, desolate and lonely, but over time, poetically at least, it has come to mean simple, unmaterialistic, humble by choice, and in tune with nature. Someone who is perfectly comfortable being himself and never craves to be anything else would be described as wabi.

Sabi means the bloom of time. It connotes natural progression—tarnish, hoariness, rust, the extinguished gloss of that which once sparkled. It's the deep philosophical understanding that beauty is fleeting. The word's meaning has also evolved over time, to the non-judgemental 'to grow old', to taking pleasure in things that were old and faded.

Leonard Koren, author of *Wabi-Sabi for Artists, Designers, Poets & Philosophers*, tried unsuccessfully to discover a precise definition while researching for the book. He eventually coined his own, which has become standard in the West: 'Wabi-sabi is the beauty of things imperfect, impermanent and incomplete, the antithesis of our classical Western notion of beauty as something perfect, enduring and monumental.'

You must be thinking, 'I know now what to call the dust pattern on top of my TV. My unmade bed is also wabi-sabi, and so is that sink full of unwashed dishes!'

Nice try!

Wabi-sabi is not a substitute for a bad job done or laziness. It is when things have journeyed through time and they wear the age and imperfections they have gathered, well. Even the most rare and expensive antiques will never suit a house that's cluttered or dirty. *Chanoyu Ichie Shu*, a tea textbook, goes as far as to advise guests to look into the host's toilet if they wish to understand his spiritual training.

In our context, we should see wabi-sabi as a celebration of creativity in every form, including the errors and failures along the way. We take inspiration from wabi-sabi to remind ourselves that there is great beauty even in imperfection.

Look up the wonderful *La Grande Odalisque* by Jean-Auguste-Dominique Ingres. If you look at the painting carefully, you will notice that the woman's thigh is almost the same size as her upper body. This is not a proportion we tend to exalt. There are studies that say her left arm is shorter than her right and her back has a few vertebrae more than an average human being. Yet, the woman looks sensual and beautiful. The painting is not in the least bit flawed by this mistake.

Once a man saw Picasso's famous painting *Les Demoiselles d'Avignon* and asked him why he didn't paint women the way they looked. Picasso asked him how women really looked, so the man showed him a picture of his wife. 'Ah! I get it,' said Picasso. 'Women are small, and black and white, and flat!'

Kintsugi, another wonderful Japanese philosophy, provides a beautiful rationale for keeping an object around even after it has broken, highlighting the cracks and repairs as simply an event in the life of an object rather than allowing its service to end at the time of its damage or breakage. Kintsugi also relates to the Japanese philosophy of no mind or *mushin*, which encompasses the concepts of detachment, acceptance of change and fate as aspects of life.

In her book *Flickwerk: The Aesthetics of Mended Japanese Ceramic*, Christy Bartlett says, 'Not only is there no attempt to hide the damage, but the repair is literally illuminated… a kind of physical expression of the spirit of *mushin*. Mushin carries connotations of fully existing within the moment, of non-attachment, of equanimity amid changing conditions. The vicissitudes of existence over time, to which all humans are susceptible, could not be clearer than in the breaks, the knocks, and the shattering to which ceramic ware too is subject. This poignancy or aesthetic of existence has been known in Japan as *mono no aware*, a compassionate sensitivity, or perhaps identification with things outside oneself.'

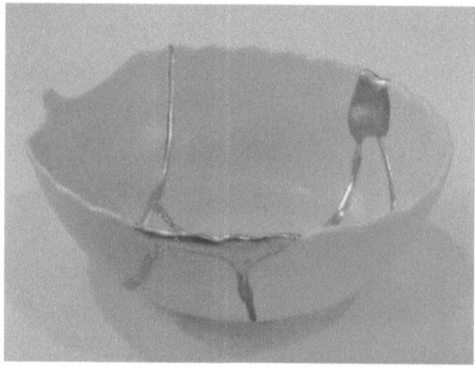

Source: Lakeside Pottery

An Adobe survey rated Japan as the most creative country in the world and Tokyo the most creative city. Why is Japan so creative? The answers are not clear. But for a lot of Japanese people, it's just the way it is!

Japan is often seen as a perfect country. This is best exemplified by the punctuality of its trains. The bullet train Tokaido Shinkansen runs 120,000 times a year with an average delay of 36 seconds.

However, from Sen no Rikyu, the tea master who designed tea cups in imperfect shapes some 500 years ago, and wabi-sabi, we see that the Japanese also find beauty in an imperfect world. Nature too is perfect and has its imperfections. Could it be in playing with this paradox that creativity arises?

In addition to perfection, discipline and order are also part of Japanese culture. During rush hour in Tokyo, people still stand neatly in line for trains. Their disciplined recovery from disasters is well chronicled. But the Japanese also have a wild side. Costume play, karaoke and drinking enable them to break out. Could there be an interplay between the adult state and the child state?

Food for contemplation!

Day 2

Exercise 1: Body Scan

Exercise 2: Letting Go of a Person or People

TIME
10 to 15 minutes (or as long as you want)

STEPS
1. Choose an object from everyday life. It could be a pebble, a piece of paper you can crumple, a cloth or even a balloon—something you are prepared to let go.

2. Sit comfortably in a chair with your back straight. Place your hands on your knees with palms facing upwards and hold the chosen object in one hand. Keep your head straight and close your eyes.
3. Recall the memory of an incident when evaluation did not work favourably for you, an instance when you strongly felt you were assessed unfairly. It could be from any period and any area of your life. It should be an incident that shook your confidence in your creative ability—perhaps a childhood drawing your teacher criticised and your classmates laughed, or a solution to a problem your boss shot down. Let it be something that evokes a reasonably strong (but not violent) emotion, and a memory you have carried in life. Relive it and the emotion as intensely as you can, holding the object in your hands, noticing the points in your body where the emotions are manifesting. Finally, pour it all into the object. When you are ready to move on, it should feel as if the object contains everything associated with that incident.
4. Continue sitting in the same position, keeping your back straight. Make sure you are comfortable and if that means adjusting a cushion under you or to support your back, that's fine. With your eyes closed, take a deep breath, as deeply as you can. Feel it going all the way in and filling up your belly. Let your lungs and rib cage expand as you feel the breath fill you all the way to your shoulders. Hold it for a moment and then gently exhale, starting from your belly to your shoulders. Repeat a few times before you return to normal breathing.
5. Now focus on the sensation of the breath. Feel it in your nostrils. What do you feel in your body as you focus on the breath? Visualise your breath as a stream, going in and out, with a beginning and an end. As you breathe in, the beginning of the stream goes all the way down into your body to the deepest place you can feel.

At this point, the end of the stream has disappeared into your nostrils. As you breathe out, the end of the stream emerges, coming out all the way until its head is at your nostrils again. Repeat this process for as long as you want, with at least four to five repetitions. The body has relaxed. The mind has also quietened.
6. Whenever you are ready, recall the memory again. Recall the emotion it comes with and your belief that it blocks your creativity. Remember, everything is now contained in the object you have injected the memory into. It is possible that you feel a lot more dispassionate about the incident as well as the object you are holding. That is perfectly fine. When you are ready, let the object go. Just drop it softly or open your hands and let it fall out. When you are ready, gently open your eyes.

Exercise 3: Writing Meditation

TIME
10 minutes of free flow writing

Follow the steps specified for writing meditation on Day 1 (page 92 onwards) using the prompt 'When I let go, I...'.

Day 3

Exercise 1: Body Scan

Exercise 2: Burning The Ghost

TIME
10 to 15 minutes (or as long as you want)

STEPS
The exercise has two parts. In the first part, think of four or five seriously creative people. They could be a creative

genius of stature or a co-worker or friend you really admire for their creativity. Write their names down.

Against each name, list the attributes you believe make that person super creative. For example, they aren't afraid of what others might say if they wore pink piggy pyjamas to a pub. Maybe they wave a friendly hello to those who snigger. So, against their name, you would write unafraid. Once you list everyone's attributes, move on to part two.

In this part, answer the question, why am I not creative? There is no limit to the number of reasons, so feel welcome to flog yourself. Answers can range from 'It's just not in my blood' to 'I'm scared I'll never compare to my friend with the pink piggy pyjamas'.

Leave enough space on these pages to add to the list, edit or make notes. You'd be surprised at how these things can expand, shrink and change shape like ghosts over time.

During this exercise, you can write slowly, thoughtfully and deliberately if that feels more comfortable to you than free flow writing.

Day 4

Exercise 1: Colouring

TIME
10 to 15 minutes (or as long as you want)

STEPS
There are four steps in this exercise. Read them all before proceeding.
1. Once you have set yourself up, with the drawing open in front of you, do the 'Getting to Ness' exercise before continuing.

2. When you feel ready, start drawing. Using a nicely sharpened pencil or a micro-tip pen, draw the outline of the diagram in your journal. Remember, the idea is to be as neat and as accurate as possible, so make sure you are not rushed or disturbed. Don't worry about the artistic quality of the outcome. If you have trouble drawing smooth lines or if the gaps between the lines are not the same everywhere, it's completely alright. Try not to get distracted by phone calls or anyone peeping over your shoulder. In fact, if possible, place a do-not-disturb sign over your head and put your phone on silent!
3. Observe your mind during the process. Does it urge you to work faster? Does it feel uncomfortable with this activity? Maybe it tells you that you're not a silly child anymore and that this is not an exercise for intelligent adults. You may or may not even finish the drawing in one sitting. There are no rules here. Spend as much time on it as you like and you'll soon start enjoying the process and will want to spend more time doing it.
4. Once the drawing is ready, start to colour it. Again, the idea is to be as neat and as accurate as possible. No marks are given for matching and coordinating colours, so let your imagination decide what feels best in the moment. You may stop at any point you feel comfortable with the time you've spent on this exercise. In the early stages of your practice, you may feel like stopping sooner than later. That too is fine. You are not being judged by the time you spend on the exercise, only by the time you feel like spending on it!

Note: You can do any number of these at any time you wish. You can create your own simple or complex patterns and drawings or get colouring books, the choice is yours. There is just one rule—make sure you do them mindfully.

In time and with practise, you'll find that this exercise carries you to a powerful existential state of no mind where you are so immersed that you slip from a state of doing into a state of being.

Here are a few more for inspiration.

Exercise 2: Writing Meditation

TIME
5 to 10 minutes (or as long as you want)

Observe any thoughts or feelings that arose in you as you did the colouring exercise and note them down in your journal. Even simple words will do. If you feel happy or calm, write that down. If you feel frustrated, write that down too. For this meditation, use the prompt, 'As I did the colouring, I...'.

Day 5

Exercise 1: Finding My Creative Genie

Creativity is much more than a mental game. It is a wonderful dance between mind and body, thoughts and feelings. Like in relaxed states, blood flows freely through the body, ideas too flow more freely, and with each exercise you will become more aware and also confident of your own creative abilities.

TIME
5 to 10 minutes (or as long as you want)

STEPS
1. Recall a time when you've been creative—you had an idea, or you solved a problem. It could be anything that's important to you, and occurred at any time. It could be how you built a secret hideaway as a kid or the way you resolved a problem at work or fixed a persistent plumbing leak at home.
2. Repeat the 'Getting to Ness' exercise.
3. Recreate the memory all over again and remember the period before you came to a solution. How did it feel? What

were the circumstances around the situation? Now, recall how the answer came to you. Relive the eureka moment. What were the conditions at the time? How did it feel when the aha came to you? What did you do next? How did you put the idea into action? What were your feelings? What was the resulting effect of your idea? Continue sitting with your eyes closed and mull over the whole experience. Whenever you are ready, gently open your eyes.

Exercise 2: Writing Meditation

TIME
5 to 10 minutes (or as long as you want)

STEPS
For this exercise, you can write slowly, thoughtfully and deliberately if that is more comfortable for you than free flow writing.

In your journal, record the incident you visualised in as much detail as possible. Try to record things like colour, sound, what people were wearing, etc. Jot down any feelings and emotions you experienced during the visualisation.

You can repeat these exercises as often as possible—you will benefit greatly from setting aside a little time each day to them. And these are some of your life's greatest moments and sharing them with a trusted friend or companion can make the process even more powerful. Pay close attention to your own spirit of creativity. By linking it to the state of mindfulness around the memory, you're unleashing a primordial energy within you. This is the supreme energy of creation!

As you repeat this exercise again and again, you might also begin to see a pattern. It could be something specific that happens to you every time you are faced with a challenge that requires a creative solution. For example, do you recognise the problem easily or not? Do you have a systematic approach to problem-solving? How do you prepare? Do you feel a lot of frustration? Is there a specific place you feel you get stuck at?

You may list any other patterns or commonalities in your journal that you might have observed in all these cases.

Day 6

Exercise 1: Getting to Ness

Exercise 2: Your Creative Genie's Diet

TIME
5 to 10 minutes (or as long as you want)

STEPS
For this exercise, you can write slowly, thoughtfully and deliberately if that is more comfortable for you than free flow writing.

Reflect on your daily life. Do you feel stressed, tense or angry a lot? Do you walk around with a clenched jaw and curled fists? Do you fly off the handle easily when you're driving? If the answer to any of these is yes, your lower brain is probably overworked.

Try to break down your day into parts. The first part could be from the time you wake up, to when you leave home or when you start work/school/college/house work—focusing on your main responsibility. What do you like about this part? What don't you like? What triggers your anxiety? What relaxes you?

Similarly, break your day into more parts and list the triggers and happy moments.

You are trying to identify your creative genie's current diet. Are you feeding it things it likes (happy and relaxed moments), or are you overdosing it with junk (all your triggers)? You can do this exercise in the beginning and keep repeating it at regular intervals on your creative journey. It can serve as a dashboard of your genie's improving health.

Day 7

Exercise 1: Genie Check-in

In this practice, you will say hello to your creative genie and check in on how he is doing. Is he awakening, saying something to you maybe? Or does he need a little more time? Whatever comes up, don't judge it. Self-compassion works wonders with genies.

A few questions that might help your genie conversation:
    How many days did you practise?
    What was easy and what wasn't?
    Were there any other feelings or thoughts that surfaced?
Use your journal to record whatever comes up.

Over time, these check-ins will also provide a blueprint of your creative journey—one you can reflect on and share if you choose to help others on their journey.

Exercise 2: Mindful Meanderings

Choose a creative space in your town or city. It could be any place that epitomises creativity for you—a gallery, museum, music school or even a café or a park. Plan to spend a leisurely amount of time here, soaking up the atmosphere and getting inspired. Carry your journal to record anything that arises. This is your creative oxygen tank. Revisit the feelings evoked on this day whenever you need an extra dose of inspiration.

13. WEEK 2: COPING WITH OUR FEAR OF FAILURE

The Fear of Failure Goblin is second-in-command of the anti-creativity army. A relative of Chief Creativity Goblin Mr Evaluation, he works closely with him to sabotage your creativity. Let's see how we can smoke him out.

Ask yourself: What all would you do if you didn't know you could fail? Stop reading, albeit briefly, to answer this question before you proceed.

I'm always amazed at what people come up with. Merely imagining the absence of failure gives people wings!

Most of us refuse to do things beyond a point or do them at all because the risk of making a mistake, or worse, failing, is just too great. But what exactly does making a mistake mean and what defines failure? Why does our fear of mistakes and failure rule over us?

Our aversion to failure and mistakes is rooted in the belief that we must adhere to a standard or plan, which is defined by the circumstances of another time, another context and a different person. This standard is called success. However, if you don't start with a rigid plan in the first place, it's hard to make a mistake.

The fear of failure also comes from mindless learning and enforcement of rules. We are supposed to have a very clear idea of the correct thing to do even before we start doing it.

Any deviation from that wonderfully clear rigid way is a mistake and you'll be beaten repeatedly with the mistake until you give up. And then, you are deemed a failure.

Perhaps you are nodding in agreement already, but that's not all. We too evaluate others, their actions and results from our rigid 'right' perspective and anything that comes from another perspective is judged to be a mistake.

In my opinion, the failure to make mistakes is the biggest failure of all. Failures and mistakes are wonderful teachers.

Failure is an opportunity to approach a problem from another angle. Remember the Zen model of creative problem-solving where you become one with the problem? When you fail to enter the problem from one door, try another. Or try the window.

Mistakes allow you to laugh at yourself. They help you discover new things without stifling yourself with pressure and seriousness. Think of perfectionists who never make mistakes and whose very glance could make us feel inadequate. Boring!

Mistakes help you evolve.

> *Ever tried. Ever failed. No matter. Try Again. Fail again. Fail better.*
>
> **Samuel Beckett**

Here's a nice story about failure.

Once upon a time, there was a farmer. He was tired of natural factors ruling the quality of his crop and consistently wanted good crop. So, one day he dialed God and said, 'Look, I am tired of all this nonsense happening in the name of nature. Obviously, you haven't been a farmer. Everything is happening at the wrong time. So, why don't you leave matters in my hands? I am a farmer and I know when it needs to rain, when there needs to be sunlight. You just leave it to me.'

God was in one of those moods, so he said, 'OK, here you go. Nature is in your hands from now on.'

The farmer planted his crop and called out, 'Rain'. And it rained. He waited until the water was soaked up to four inches and said, 'Stop'. He ploughed his field and planted maize seeds and waited for a few days. Rain then sunlight followed perfectly.

One day he was working in the field and felt hot, so he summoned clouds. By then, the farmer was remotely managing everything from home. Soon a beautiful crop of maize came up and he was overjoyed. It was time for harvest. He went down to the fields to reap, but when he looked at the crop, he was shocked. There was no grain on the plants! 'What the hell, what did I do wrong?' he thought. After all, he had managed nature perfectly with zero mistakes.

He called God again and asked, 'I did everything perfectly but there is no grain. Have you been up to something?' God said, 'No way, man. I've only been watching you. You were the boss, so I didn't interfere. The rain was perfect, the sunshine was perfect, everything was perfect, but you stopped the winds. You see, I used to send strong winds that would threaten your crop, and because the plants felt vulnerable, they put their roots deeper into earth and produced grain so they could continue to survive as a species. Now, you have a great crop but no maize.'

At IDEO, there is a saying: Fail early to succeed soon. People are encouraged to try new things quickly in cheap and dirty ways so they can fail and figure out better ways of doing things. In other words, evolve and move on.

History is also replete with stories of people overcoming mistakes, odds, failures and accidents to rise above the ordinary. How did they do it? Were they all born without a fear of failure? Probably not. They simply overcame it.

Courage is not the absence of fear, but rather the assessment that something else is more important than the fear.

Franklin Roosevelt

Now, for the big question—how do we use mindfulness to overcome this fear?

The first step is to recognise that fear and courage are not separate. There is no realm where only courage exists or only fear exists. But don't despair, because it is only when there's one that the other can exist. In fact, there is a lesser-known story about when God created Earth and said, 'Let there be light.' Apparently light said, 'I'll wait for my twin darkness, for without him, I don't exist.'

Often, when there is fear, we think that's all there is. We think courage belongs to another time, another place or another person. Imagining life without fear is as delusional as conceiving right without left. Where there is courage, there is fear, and where there is fear, there is courage.

And so, in true ninja style, the next step in overcoming the fear of failure is to identify the fear and embrace it. Embracing your fear seems like the opposite of what we want to do, but non-judgementally recognising and embracing it is not the same as giving in to it. Once you acknowledge and care for the fear, it will become less scary and powerful. For most of us, there are at least a few voices in our heads at any point in time. One brings up the past, another worries about the unknown future and a third berates us for all that we haven't done right. These feed our fear. We dwell on the past, feel sadness and regret and repeatedly obsess over our fears and pains. We consume mindless media, gossip or food in an attempt to ignore them or distract ourselves. Instead, we end up getting addicted to the things that not only fail to address ours fears, but fuel it through stories and images of greed, craving, power, etc. They numb us briefly, only to make us feel worse in time.

If we quieten or silence these voices, we can slowly starve the Fear of Failure goblin and weaken it. As we call upon the energy of mindfulness to embrace the goblin, courage comes forth automatically.

What all would you do if you didn't think you would fail?

Renew your intent for the week by repeating your declaration to the universe in the beginning of Part B.

Day 1

Exercise 1: Body Scan

Exercise 2: Hello Failure—Embracing a Situation

STEPS
1. Ideally, this is to be written. When you are ready, recall one horror story where you made a mistake or failed in a creative endeavour. This memory has to be of an incident where you acknowledged failure. Write it down. Jot down all the details that come to mind. The day, time, where you were, what you were wearing, the room you were in, the way people looked at you, the way you felt, what people said, what you felt they didn't say, what you said, what you didn't say… everything that still upsets and hurts you. A sample sentence would be: 'Everyone laughed and I realised I had got the instructions wrong. My cheeks burned, and I wished the earth would open up and swallow me.'

If you want to write the story first and then embellish it with drawings, do that. If you want to draw a failure monster with horns perched high on a wall, chuckling at you, even better.

Notice any sensations that arise in your body. Is there a tightening of the chest or the gut or hunched shoulders? Be aware of any emotions manifesting themselves in the body.

2. Sit comfortably on a chair with your back straight. Place your palms on your knees, keep your head straight and close your eyes. Take three deep inhalations and exhalations, or as many as you like until you feel calm and aware.

Breathing in, I know I have fears; breathing out, I say hello to my fears.
Breathing in, I know I have fears; breathing out, I say hello to my fears.
Breathing in, I know I have fears; breathing out, I say hello to my fears.

You will now reunite your mind and body and arrive in the present moment. With each breath, you'll generate mindful energy that creates a caring acknowledgement of your fears. In a few minutes of such mindful breathing accompanied by the affirmation, you may notice regrets about the past have paused and uncertainty, fear and worries about the future have reduced.

Breathing mindfully is not terribly hard to do. You breathe all the time, now you just do it consciously for a while. Thich Nhat Hanh says, 'Mindful breathing is like the morning sunshine on a flower that has closed overnight. The sunshine just embraces and subtly permeates the flower. Embraced by the energy of the sunshine, the flower begins to bloom.'

3. Slowly, consciously, when you are ready, in your mind's eye, recall the incident you just wrote about. Embrace it.

In a state of mindfulness, you might be able to see it differently and not as the calamity you thought it to be. You may understand why it happened the way it happened. Perhaps you didn't hear the instructions you were given that day or you were just distracted. Whatever reason comes to you in that moment, embrace it. Try to view the incident as something that simply happened and not judge it as good or bad. Reflect on what can be learnt from it. Do this as long as it is comfortable for you and you continue to remain mindful and non-judgemental.

Here is a little secret. As a deep awareness of the true nature of the episode comes to you, a gentle smile might come to your lips. The absurdity of having been chained by this incident may seem vaguely amusing. Be magnanimous in the moment, for without fear, there is no courage. When the light comes, thank the darkness for doing its job and then, let it fade. Use the energy of your mindfulness to become aware of the areas in the body where any emotions had manifested earlier. By taking your awareness to the sensation or that part of the body, allow it to dissolve. When you are ready, gently open your eyes.

As with the other exercises, you may repeat this one too as many times as you like, until you feel you have greater control over the Fear of Failure Goblin.

Day 2

Exercise 1: Body Scan

Exercise 2: Hello Failure—Accepting a Person

STEPS
1. Ideally, this is to be written. When you are ready, recall one horror story where you made a mistake or failed in a creative endeavour. It should be an incident where a person classified you as a failure, in public or private.

Write it down. Jot down all the details that come to mind. The day, time, where you were, what you were wearing, the room you were in, the way people looked at you, the way you felt, what people said, what you felt they didn't say, what you said, what you didn't say… everything that still upsets and hurts you. 'You are a loser', 'You are so dumb', or 'You don't get it' are all allowed.

If you want to write the story first and then embellish it with drawings, do that. If you want to draw a failure monster with horns perched high on a wall, chuckling at you, even better.

Notice any sensations that arise in your body. Is there a tightening of the chest or the gut or hunched shoulders? Be aware of any emotions manifesting themselves in the body.

2. Sit comfortably on a chair with your back straight. Place your palms on your knees, keep your head straight and close your eyes. Take three deep inhalations and exhalations, or as many as you like until you feel calm and aware.

Breathing in, I know I have fears; breathing out, I say hello to my fears.
Breathing in, I know I have fears; breathing out, I say hello to my fears.
Breathing in, I know I have fears; breathing out, I say hello to my fears.

You will now reunite your mind and body and arrive in the present moment. With each breath, you'll generate mindful energy that creates a caring acknowledgement of your fears. In a few minutes of such mindful breathing accompanied by the affirmation, you may notice regrets about the past have paused and uncertainty, fear and worries about the future have reduced.

3. Slowly, consciously, when you are ready, in your mind's eye, recall the incident you just wrote about. Embrace it. In a state of mindfulness, you might be able to see it differently and not as the calamity you thought it to be. You may understand why it happened the way it happened. Perhaps the person who hurt you was having a bad day or being who they are. Can you forgive them? Whatever answer comes to you in that moment, embrace it. Try to view the incident as something that simply happened and not judge it as good or bad. Reflect on what can be learnt from it. Do this as long as it is comfortable for you and you continue to remain mindful and non-judgemental.

   As a deep awareness of the true nature of the episode comes to you, a gentle smile might come to your lips. The absurdity of having been chained by this incident may seem vaguely amusing. Be magnanimous in the moment, for without fear, there is no courage. When the light comes, thank the darkness for doing its job and then, let it fade. Use the energy of your mindfulness to become aware of the areas in the body where any emotions had manifested earlier. By taking your awareness to the sensation or that part of the body, allow it to dissolve. When you are ready, gently open your eyes.

   As with the other exercises, you may repeat this one too as many times as you like, until you feel you have greater control over the Fear of Failure Goblin.

9 STEPS TO FORGIVENESS

Dr Fred Luskin runs the Stanford Forgiveness Project, the largest interpersonal forgiveness training research project ever done. He offers this advice:

1. You have to know *exactly* how you feel about what happened and be able to articulate what is not OK. Talk to a trusted person about your experience.
2. Make a commitment to yourself to feel better. Forgiveness is for you and no one else.
3. Forgiveness does not necessarily mean reconciling with the person who upset you or condoning their action; you seek peace and the understanding that comes from blaming people less and taking those offences less personally.
4. Get the right perspective on what is happening. Recognise that your primary distress is coming from hurt feelings and thoughts that you are suffering now, not from what hurt you 10 years ago.
5. The moment you feel upset, practise stress management to soothe your body's fight-or-flight response.
6. Give up expecting things from your life or from other people that they do not choose to give you.
8. Put your energy into looking for another way to get your positive goals met than through the experience that has hurt you.
8. Remember that a life well lived is your best revenge.
9. Amend the way you look at your past, so you remind yourself of your heroic choice to forgive.

Day 3

Exercise 1: Getting to Ness

Exercise 2: Calling Upon Courage

STEPS
1. Recall and write one happy episode where you were a hero, where you did something brave and successful. It could be a situation where you saved the milk from the cat or nabbed a robber or said/made something that was well-appreciated.
   Like in the earlier exercises, this memory has to be recreated in detail. So, jot down all the details that come to mind—time, day, date, place, people, colours, clothes, feelings, thoughts, emotions, etc.
2. Sit comfortably on a chair with your back straight. Place your palms on your knees, keep your head straight and close your eyes. Take three deep inhalations and exhalations, or as many as you like until you feel calm and aware.
   Breathing in, I know I have fears; breathing out, I also have courage.
   Breathing in, I know I have fears; breathing out, I also have courage.
   Breathing in, I know I have fears; breathing out, I also have courage.
3. Slowly, consciously, when you are ready, in your mind's eye, recall the incident you wrote about. Embrace it, and in a state of mindfulness, declare your intent to create more such situations. Declare an intent to be more generous with your courage. We all need a few heroes around. How can you be somebody's (or maybe your own) secret hero? Let the intent be one of courageously helping oneself and others in all humility. A word of caution: Don't let this

mindful declaration of your courage intention get mixed up with brazen chest-thumping in-your-face heroism. When you are ready, gently open your eyes.

As with the other exercises, repeat this one too as many times as you like.

Day 4

Exercise 1: Manifesting My Best Me

TIME
10 to 15 minutes (or as long as you want)

STEPS
1. With your eyes closed, create an image of you in your most successful avatar, whatever that's like for you. It could include a title (CEO), a role (spouse/parent), material goals (car, money, etc.) and even emotional goals (calmness, happiness, etc.).
As in all our exercises, make it detailed.
2. Perform the 'Getting to Ness' exercise.
3. When you are ready, gently open your eyes. In five minutes, write everything that seems important from your visualisation of your most successful avatar. Go free flow or slow and thoughtful, whatever is comfortable for you.

Day 5

Exercise 1: Walking Meditation

Exercise 2: Make Something. Anything.

TIME
30 to 60 minutes

STEPS

It could be a stick figure made of twigs, a boomerang or a painting, as long as you make something with your hands. You are allowed to do research, look for inspiration, download instructions, etc. Just remember that it should be an activity during which you don't multitask, and preferably something that can be completed in one sitting of 30 to 60 minutes. No gadgets will enhance the benefits of this exercise. You don't get marks for the outcome, only for the quality of the effort.

Day 6

Exercise 1: Walking Meditation

Exercise 2: Make Something. Anything.

Tip: Cook a dish, make an arrangement in the garden or create a handmade card for someone. Make something out of recycled material. Avoid gadgets and multitasking, and remember to stay non-judgemental and enjoy the process!

Day 7

Exercise 1: Genie Check-in

In this practice, you will say hello to your creative genie and check in on how he is doing. Is he awakening, saying something to you maybe? Or does he need a little more time? Whatever comes up, don't judge it. Self-compassion works wonders with genies.

A few questions that might help your genie conversation:
How many days did you practise?
What was easy and what wasn't?
Were there any other feelings or thoughts that surfaced?
Use your journal to record whatever comes up.

Over time, these check-ins will also provide a blueprint of your creative journey—one you can reflect on and share if you choose to help others on their journey.

Exercise 2: Mindful Meanderings

Choose a creative space in your town or city. It could be any place that epitomises creativity for you—a gallery, museum, music school or even a café or a park. Plan to spend a leisurely amount of time here, soaking up the atmosphere and getting inspired. Carry your journal to record anything that arises. This is your creative oxygen tank. Revisit the feelings evoked on this day whenever you need an extra dose of inspiration.

14. WEEK 3: WORKING WITH THE LIMITATIONS OF RULES

Know the rules well, so you can break them effectively.

Dalai Lama

This week, we take on the strict and formidable goblin Mr Rules.

Let's start by understanding what a rule means.

Picking from Merriam Webster's definitions, a rule could be any of the following.

1. A prescribed guide for conduct or action
2. An accepted procedure, custom, or habit
3. (a) A usually valid generalisation
   (b) A generally prevailing quality, state or mode
4. A standard of judgment: criterion
5. A regulating principle

In summary, a rule is an accepted way of doing things.

However, creativity is doing something new, and how can you do something new by doing it the same old way?

That too, without error. In turn, our aversion to error is often the result of the mindless learning and application of rules. While it is certainly good to have an idea of the right way of doing things, it is in challenging it that a new way appears. Similarly, taking conditional information and imposing certainty on it also leads to the assumption that any deviation is a mistake.

If you want something new, you have to stop doing something old.

Peter Drucker

Let's explore the importance of a beginner's mind, a mind that doesn't know.

> 'In the beginner's mind there are many possibilities, but in the expert's there are few.
>
> People say that practising Zen is difficult, but there is a misunderstanding as to why. It is not difficult because it is hard to sit in the cross-legged position, or attain enlightenment. It is difficult because it is hard to keep our mind pure and our practice pure in its fundamental sense...
>
> In Japan, we have the phrase *shoshin*, which means beginner's mind. The goal of practice is to always keep our beginner's mind. Suppose you recite the Prajna Paramita Sutra only once. It might be a very good recitation, but what would happen if you recited it twice, three times, four times or more? You might easily lose your original attitude towards it. The same thing

will happen in your other Zen practices. For a while you will keep your beginner's mind, but if you continue to practise one, two, three years or more, although you may improve some, you're liable to lose the limitless meaning of the original mind.

For Zen students, the most important thing is not to be dualistic. Our original mind includes everything within itself. It is always rich and sufficient within itself. You should not lose your self-sufficient state of mind. This does not mean a closed mind, but actually an empty mind and a ready mind. If your mind is empty, it is always ready for anything, it is open to everything. In the beginner's mind there are many possibilities; in the expert's mind there are few...

In the beginner's mind, there is no thought, "I have attained something." All self-centred thoughts limit our vast mind. When we have no thought of achievement or self, we are true beginners. Then we can really learn something. The beginner's mind is a mind of compassion. When our mind is compassionate, it is boundless. Dogen-zenji, the founder of our school, always emphasised how important it is to resume our boundless original mind. Then we are always true to ourselves, in sympathy with all beings, and can actually practise.

So, the most difficult thing is always to keep your beginner's mind. There is no need to have a deep understanding of Zen. Even though you read much Zen literature, you must read each sentence with a fresh mind. You should not say, "I know what Zen is", or "I have attained enlightenment".

This is also the real secret of the arts: Always be a beginner.'

From *Zen Mind, Beginner's Mind* by Shunryu Suzuki

If you don't know what you are doing, you don't know what you can't do!

When you don't know something completely, it is then that you don't see yourself as making mistakes. You see yourself as a learner. On the other hand, when you know something really well, you might be well unaware of how much you don't know about it.

John Gardner writes in *The Art of Fiction*: 'Art depends heavily on feeling, intuition, taste. It is feeling, not some rule, that tells the abstract painter to put his yellow here and there, not there, and may later tell him that it should have been brown, purple or pea-green. It is feeling that makes the composer break surprisingly from his key, feeling that gives the writer the rhythms of his sentences, the pattern of rise and fall in his episodes, the proportions of alternating elements, so that dialogue goes on only so long before a shift to description or narrative summary or some physical action.'

What Gardner points out is that feeling, intuition and taste are what spark creativity. Looking at the world through logical spreadsheets could eliminate mistakes, but it also reduces creativity.

Mindfulness makes you aware of feeling and intuition. It helps you accept uncertainty by keeping you in the present moment. And the present moment is the only certainty. So, the next time we evaluate or judge another individual's thinking or actions as mistakes, let's stop for a moment to understand if they had a different perspective.

> *Mistakes are almost always of a sacred nature. Never try to correct them. On the contrary: Rationalise them, understand them thoroughly. After that, it will be possible for you to sublimate them.*
>
> Salvador Dali

Renew your intent for the week by repeating your declaration to the universe at the beginning of Part B.

All the journaling exercises this week are meant to be done in a reflective manner and unlike the spontaneous, free flow writing meditations we did in previous weeks.

Day 1

Exercise 1: Walking Meditation

Exercise 2: Circle of Life

TIME
30 to 60 minutes

This exercise is meant to make you reflect on your life as it is right now, to create an awareness of how things are in different aspects. Then, it gets you to improve the areas you identify. What does this have do with creativity? Remember Law 9 of the creativity laws—we are creating a healthy state of being.

You could try drawing this out in your creativity journal and then follow the steps of the exercise to make your notes alongside the figure.

Your name: Date:

STEPS

Reflect on the eight categories. Think about what a satisfying life might look like for you in each area.

Next, draw a line across each segment/category that reflects your satisfaction score for each area.

Imagine the centre of the wheel is zero and the outer edge is 10. Choose a value between one (very dissatisfied) and 10 (fully satisfied). Now draw a line and write the score alongside (see example). Use the first number that pops into your head, not the number you think it *should* be.

Note: This is unique to each individual. It allows you to plan your life better and make it more satisfying. It also helps set goals in different areas. So, don't compare with another person; see how your circle evolves with time. Check in regularly with this circle and learn more about yourself. If there's someone you trust wholeheartedly and whose opinion you value, it's a good idea to get them to fill this for you—their perception of your life—as it will add more perspective for you.

Feel free to split category segments to add something that is missing, or relabel an area to make it more meaningful for you. Here are some examples:

Family and Friends: You could split them into separate categories.
Spouse/Partner: You could change it to Relationship or Life Partner.
Career: Change this to Motherhood, Work, Business or Job.
Money: Change to Finance, Financial Security or Financial Well-being.
Health: You can split this up or change to Emotional, Physical, Fitness, Spiritual or Well-being.
Home Environment: Split or change to Work Environment for career or business.

Personal Growth: Rename as Learning, Self-Development or Spiritual.

Other categories you can add are Security, Service, Leadership, Achievement and Community. Once you complete your circle, step back and look at it. What does the path made by connecting the lines look like? Is it smooth or bumpy?

Here's what it might look like.

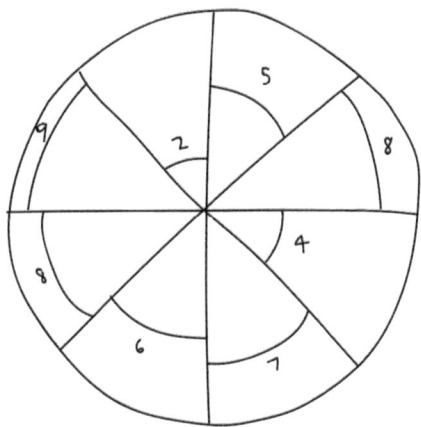

Answer the following questions to go deeper.
1. Did anything surprise you?
2. How does your life feel as you look at this circle? What kind of overall score do you feel you have?
3. What kind of a score in each category would make you feel good?
4. Which categories would you like to improve?
5. What changes would you like to make in each category?
6. What help and support do you think you need?
7. Where do you think you should start?
8. If there was one key action you could take to bring everything into balance, what would that be?

Finally, pick one or two action points for each area you'll work on every week over the next eight weeks or more.

Day 2

Exercise 1: Walking Meditation

Exercise 2: In your creativity journal, list five people you admire and who you think live life expansively.

They could be characterised by high spirits, generosity and energy. You could even use the 'Circle of Life' exercise to see who scores high in your perspective. How have these characteristics manifested in their lives and in the different categories? Highlight some you would like for yourself.

Day 3

Exercise 1: Walking Meditation

Exercise 2: In your creativity journal, list five things about yourself that are unconventional or which you consider different and are proud of.

What makes you different from others?

Day 4

Exercise 1: Getting to Ness

Exercise 2: Write a letter from your future self from 15 years later to your current self.

What would your older self say to you now?

Day 5

Exercise 1: Getting to Ness

Exercise 2: Reorganise the space where you spend most of your time.

It could be your office cubicle, a corner of your home or your room. Bring in elements that would inspire you to live at your creative best, whatever that means for you.

Day 6

Exercise 1: Getting to Ness

Exercise 2: Since this is the week of rules, we also respect rules. After all, we have been playing with paradoxes right through this book.

Create six rules you would like to have—rules that give you a sense of purpose and freedom, and which energise you. For example, 'I will not say yes when I mean no', or 'I will bring a sense of passion and purpose into everything I do'.

Day 7

Exercise 1: Genie Check-in

In this practice, you will say hello to your creative genie and check in on how he is doing. Is he awakening, saying something to you maybe? Or does he need a little more time? Whatever comes up, don't judge it. Self-compassion works wonders with genies.

A few questions that might help your genie conversation:
  How many days did you practise?
  What was easy and what wasn't?
  Were there any other feelings or thoughts that surfaced?
Use your journal to record whatever comes up.

Over time, these check-ins will also provide a blueprint of your creative journey—one you can reflect on and share if you choose to help others on their journey.

Exercise 2: Mindful Meanderings

Choose a creative space in your town or city. It could be any place that epitomises creativity for you—a gallery, museum, music school or even a café or a park. Plan to spend a leisurely amount of time here, soaking up the atmosphere and getting inspired. Carry your journal to record anything that arises. This is your creative oxygen tank. Revisit the feelings evoked on this day whenever you need an extra dose of inspiration.

15. WEEK 4: EMBRACING THE PAIN OF COMPARISONS

This week, we meet the next goblin—the Fear of Comparison Goblin.

I used to coach a young marketing manager called Ana. One day I found her in a rather despondent mood. After conversing with her for a few minutes, the reason became evident. Ana had been on Facebook while waiting for me to join her, and saw her friend's picture next to a painting she had made. The post had garnered many likes and comments. Ana was left feeling completely uncreative and defeated. Sounds familiar?

It's not just us who compare ourselves poorly to others. There are people in our lives who are also guilty of the crime—teachers, parents, siblings, colleagues, bosses, partners. The list is endless.

Why does this happen to so many of us? Why are we so quick to fall into the trap of comparison? On the other hand, comparison also sometimes inspires us. So, how then do we differentiate between healthy and unhealthy comparison and use the right motivators to become more creative? Is it possible that when we see others achieve something through sheer grit and effort, we find it inspiring, but when we attribute their achievement to inborn talent or creativity, we find it unattainable and demoralising?

There is a large amount of psychological research that deals with evaluations and comparisons. Several theories also assume that people will make evaluations and comparisons. I, however, submit that we can give up mindless evaluations, which inhibit our creativity, and instead realise that everything is fine just the way it is through the practice of mindfulness.

Don't get me wrong. Comparison is natural and, in the right context, even important. It can be a great way to learn as long as we remain aware. Unfortunately, there is a lot of social comparison, which is simply unhelpful. We often end up comparing ourselves to those who are less able, only to falsely boost our self-image. In reality, this is only setting us up for future unhappiness because just around the corner is someone who is better than we are.

'Oh my God, I need to be Buddha to achieve this state' is probably what you are thinking. Without denying this, what if you had a better sense of the implications of the comparisons you make? What if you realised deep within that the damage you cause to yourself by allowing these constant comparisons is much worse than the pain of the comparison itself? Mindfulness helps you do exactly that.

Everybody is a genius. But if you judge a fish by its ability to climb a tree, it will live its whole life believing that it is stupid.

Albert Einstein

After practising mindfulness for a few weeks, Ana came up to me one day and said, 'Hey G, do you remember the day I was really upset because Maya had posted a picture of herself with her painting on Facebook? Well, I realised something. And so, stuff like that doesn't bother me anymore.'

'Wow Ana, what did you realise?' I asked.

'I am the only person who can ever be me,' she said, with a twinkle in her eye.

> A crow lived in a forest and was absolutely satisfied. But one day, he saw a swan. 'This swan is so white,' he thought, 'and I am so black. This swan must be the happiest bird in the world.' He expressed his thoughts to the swan. 'Actually,' he replied, 'I was the happiest bird until I saw a parrot, which has two colours. I now think the parrot is the happiest bird in creation.'
>
> The crow then approached the parrot. The parrot explained, 'I lived a very happy life until I saw a peacock. I have only two colours, but the peacock has multiple colours.' Then the crow visited a peacock in the zoo and saw that hundreds of people had gathered to see him. After they left, the crow approached him. 'Dear peacock,' he said, 'you are so beautiful. Every day thousands of people come to see you. When people see me, they immediately shoo me away. I think you are the happiest bird on the planet.'
>
> The peacock replied, 'I always thought that I was the happiest and most beautiful bird on the planet. But because of my beauty, I am trapped in this zoo. I have examined the zoo carefully, and I have realised that the crow is the only bird not kept in a cage. So, I've been thinking that if I were a crow, I could happily roam everywhere.'

Renew your intent for the week by repeating your declaration to the universe at the beginning of Part B.

All the journaling exercises this week are meant to be done in a reflective manner and unlike the spontaneous, free flow writing meditations we did in previous weeks.

Day 1

Exercise 1: Breath Awareness Meditation

Exercise 2: Draw up a memory of an unfavourable comparison made by another person and respond to them.

TIME
5 to 10 minutes

STEPS
1. Close your eyes. Remember an instance of unfavourable comparison made by another person that led to frustration, anger or pain. Try not to recall a deeply traumatic event but something that is mildly upsetting yet the memory of which gives rise to real emotion. Visualise the event and relive it in as much detail as possible. Notice where the emotion arises in your body.
2. Take your awareness to your breath. Imagine you are doing this immediately after the moment of comparison. Instead of reacting, you are now focusing your mind on your breath. Take a few more deep breaths for the next minute or so.

   Carry your awareness to where the negative emotion manifested in your body. Experience the sensation deeply. What is it like? Is it a tingling—perhaps in the face—or a tightness in the gut? A general flushed feeling, or something else?

   What's important is to experience it without judging it, as something happening in the body in a dispassionate sort of way. Instead of 'I am hurt', it is 'I experience a

sensation of hurt in my body'. Take a minute to continue experiencing the emotions in the body.
3. Now, put yourself in the shoes of the person who made the comparison. Think about the possibility that they made the comparison to make you better or make themselves happier. Without judging, just dwell in this perspective for a minute.

   Take a deep breath and bring to mind a response that will create a positive outcome in this situation. You don't have to say or do anything, just formulate the most positive response that comes to you. What is it like—the words, tone, the expression on your face? Take a minute to detail that response in your mind.
4. Take your awareness back to your breathing and take a few deep breaths. If you are still experiencing any strong sensations in your body, just direct your breath or awareness to it, allowing it to dissolve. As it does, take your awareness back to your breathing and allow your mind to settle there. Finally, when you are ready, open your eyes and bring your attention back to wherever you are.

Day 2

Exercise 1: Breath Awareness Meditation

Exercise 2: Draw up a memory of an unfavourable comparison made by yourself and respond to yourself.

TIME
5 to 10 minutes

STEPS
1. Close your eyes. Bring to mind the memory of an unfavourable comparison made by you that led to frustration, anger or pain. A time when you compared

yourself poorly with someone else or compared your outcome poorly with someone else's outcome or result. Try not to recall a deeply traumatic event but something that is mildly upsetting yet the memory of which gives rise to real emotion. Visualise the event and relive it in as much detail as possible. Notice where the emotion arises in your body.

2. Take your awareness to your breath. Imagine you are doing this immediately after the moment of comparison. Instead of reacting, you are now focusing your mind on your breath. Take a few more deep breaths for the next minute or so.

   Carry your awareness to where the negative emotion manifested in your body. Experience the sensation deeply. What is it like? Is it a tingling—perhaps in the face—or a tightness in the gut? A general flushed feeling, or something else?

   What's important is to experience it without judging it, as something happening in the body in a dispassionate sort of way. Instead of 'I am hurt', it is 'I experience a sensation of hurt in my body'. Take a minute to continue experiencing the emotions in the body.

   Think about the statement: Everybody is unique. Without judging, just dwell in this perspective for a minute.

3. Take a deep breath and bring to mind a response that will create a positive outcome in this situation. You don't have to say or do anything, just formulate the most positive response that comes to you. What is it like—the words, tone, the expression on your face? Take a minute to detail that response in your mind.

4. Take your awareness back to your breathing and take a few deep breaths. If you are still experiencing any strong sensations in your body, just direct your breath or awareness to it, allowing it to dissolve. As it does, take your awareness back to your breathing and allow

your mind to settle there. Finally, when you are ready, open your eyes and bring your attention back to wherever you are.

Day 3

Exercise 1: Breath Awareness Meditation

Exercise 2: Writing Meditation

TIME
10 minutes

As you have done many times already, you are writing just for yourself. You don't have to share anything you don't want to. In this exercise, you have 10 minutes to write free flowing about whatever comes to you. Just keep the pen moving and surprise yourself. For today, use the prompt, 'If I were my best friend or mentor, I...'. Write what you would say to yourself about healthy and unhealthy comparisons in your life.

Day 4

Exercise 1: Breath Awareness Meditation

Exercise 2: Make a list of 10 things you are good at and write down the last time you did them. Examples: singing, baking, playing a sport, motivating someone, etc.

Day 5

Exercise 1: Breath Awareness Meditation

Exercise 2: Do five things you are good at, from the list of Day 4.

Day 6

Exercise 1: Breath Awareness Meditation

Exercise 2: Do the remaining five things you listed on Day 4.

Day 7

Exercise 1: Genie Check-in

In this practice, you will say hello to your creative genie and check in on how he is doing. Is he awakening, saying something to you maybe? Or does he need a little more time? Whatever comes up, don't judge it. Self-compassion works wonders with genies.

A few questions that might help your genie conversation:
How many days did you practise?
What was easy and what wasn't?
Were there any other feelings or thoughts that surfaced? Use your journal to record whatever comes up.

Over time, these check-ins will also provide a blueprint of your creative journey—one you can reflect on and share if you choose to help others on their journey.

Exercise 2: Mindful Meanderings

Choose a creative space in your town or city. It could be any place that epitomises creativity for you—a gallery, museum, music school or even a café or a park. Plan to spend a leisurely amount of time here, soaking up the atmosphere and getting inspired. Carry your journal to record anything that arises. This is your creative oxygen tank. Revisit the feelings evoked on this day whenever you need an extra dose of inspiration.

16. WEEK 5: UNDERSTANDING THE MYTH OF TALENT

The next goblin is the one who feeds the myth called talent. I just don't have the talent for this—how often have we heard this? You either have it or you don't—how often we have all been told that!

So, I ask you, did all the talented people out there or the ones who have it know they had it before they started, or were they willing to start and see where things go? Meditate on this.

We mortals tend to focus on what creative geniuses produced and completely ignore the struggles, failures and perseverance they brought to their pursuits. What made the outcomes possible was a combination of skills, even assuming there is something inborn called talent. So, in constantly feeding the myth of talent, we keep widening the gap between them and us, and at some point completely forget about the skills that also contributed to the outcome.

If people knew how hard I worked to get my mastery, it wouldn't seem so wonderful at all.

Michelangelo

Walt Disney was fired from *The Kansas City Star* in 1919 because his editor said he 'lacked imagination and had no good ideas'. Thanks to his courage and consistency, Disney went on to purchase ABC in 1996, which at the time, owned the newspaper. The publication that once fired him became part of the empire he created. Disney learned much through his many trials and setbacks. Only when we view his story in hindsight can we understand the true meaning of perseverance. Thankfully, he had unwavering faith in his big vision.

> *Genius is one per cent inspiration, ninety-nine per cent perspiration.*
>
> Thomas Alva Edison

JK Rowling, before she became monumentally famous as the author of the legendary series of Harry Potter books, had been fired from the London office of Amnesty International because she wrote stories about a teenage wizard all day long.

In his early days, after a performance at Nashville's Grand Ole Opry, Elvis Presley was told by the concert hall manager that he was better off returning to Memphis and driving trucks.

In the first two decades of his career, Claude Monet's work was mocked and rejected by the artistic elite. He said, 'My rejection at the Salon brought an end to my hesitation (to settle in Paris) since after this failure I can no longer claim to cope... alas, that fatal rejection has virtually taken the bread out of my mouth.' Monet eventually gained a strong ally in the dealer Paul Durand-Ruel, who supported him by purchasing paintings outright while trying to attract buyers from among the newly affluent bourgeoisie for his revolutionary work. This long road to acceptance took many years to travel, but Monet persisted, never wavering from his commitment to his art.

History is replete with examples of such people who overcame discouragement and achieved great heights of creativity and success. A certain amount of discouragement is inevitable in life and in creativity, this is no exception. In some ways it serves the good purpose of inspiring improvement. Competition can also be seen the same way. Playing a game with a better player makes us play harder and can improve our skills.

But creativity comes with sensitivity and that is a double-edged sword. The same sensitivity that fuels artistic ability can lead to taking criticism very hard! Any rejection can seem like judgement on capabilities and stifle the effort even before it matures.

One day, it occurred to a certain emperor that if he only knew the answers to three questions, he would never stray in any matter.

1. What is the best time to do each thing?
2. Who are the most important people to work with?
3. What is the most important thing to do at all times?

The emperor issued a decree throughout his kingdom announcing that whoever could answer the questions would receive a great reward. Many who read the decree made their way to the palace at once, each person with a different answer.

In reply to the first question, one person advised that the emperor make up a thorough time schedule, consecrating every hour, day, month and year for certain tasks and then follow the schedule to the letter. Only then could he hope to do every task at the right time. Another person replied that it was impossible to plan in advance and that the emperor should put all vain amusements aside and remain attentive to everything in order to know what to do at what time. Someone else insisted that, by himself, the emperor could never hope to have all the foresight and competence necessary to decide when to do each and every task, and what he really needed was to set up a Council of the Wise and then to act according to their advice. Someone else said that certain matters require immediate decision and could not wait for consultation, but if he wanted to know in advance what was going to happen he should consult magicians and soothsayers.

The responses to the second question also lacked accord. One person said that the emperor needed to place all his trust in administrators, another urged reliance on priests and monks, while others recommended physicians. Still others put their faith in warriors.

The third question drew a similar variety of answers. Some said science was the most important pursuit. Others insisted on religion. Yet others claimed the most important thing was military skill.

The emperor was not pleased with any of the answers, and no reward was given. After several nights of reflection, the emperor resolved to visit a hermit who lived on a mountain and was said to be an enlightened man. The emperor wished to find the hermit to ask him the three questions, though he knew the hermit never left the mountains and was known to receive only the poor, refusing to have anything to do with persons of wealth or power. So, the emperor disguised himself as a simple peasant and ordered his attendants to wait for him at the foot of the mountain while he climbed the slope alone to seek the hermit.

Reaching the holy man's dwelling place, the emperor found the hermit digging a garden in front of his hut.

When the hermit saw the stranger, he nodded his head in greeting and continued to dig. The labour was obviously hard on him. He was an old man, and each time he thrust his spade into the ground to turn the earth, he heaved heavily.

The emperor approached him and said, 'I have come here to ask your help with three questions: When is the best time to do each thing? Who are the most important people to work with? What is the most important thing to do at all times?'

The hermit listened attentively but only patted the emperor on the shoulder and continued digging. The emperor said, 'You must be tired. Here, let me give you a hand with that.' The hermit thanked him, handed the emperor the spade, and then sat down on the ground to rest. After he had dug two rows, the emperor stopped and turned to the hermit and repeated his three questions. The hermit still did not answer, but instead stood and pointed to the spade and said, 'Why don't you rest now? I can take over again.' But the emperor continued to dig.

One hour passed, then two. Finally, the sun began to set behind the mountain. The emperor put down the spade and said to the hermit, 'I came here to ask if you could answer my three questions. But if you can't give me any answer, please let me know so that I can get on my way home.'

The hermit lifted his head and asked the emperor, 'Do you hear someone running over there?'

The emperor turned his head. They both saw a man with a long white beard emerge from the woods. He ran wildly, pressing his hands against a bloody wound in his stomach. The man ran toward the emperor before falling unconscious to the ground, where he lay groaning. Opening the man's clothing, the emperor and hermit saw that the man had received a deep gash. The emperor cleaned the wound thoroughly and then used his own shirt to bandage it, but the blood completely soaked it within minutes. He rinsed the shirt out and bandaged the wound a second time and continued to do so until the flow of blood had stopped. At last the wounded man regained consciousness and asked for a drink of water. The emperor ran down to the stream and brought back a jug of fresh water.

Meanwhile, the sun had disappeared and the night air had begun to turn cold. The hermit gave the emperor a hand in carrying the man into the hut where they laid him down on the hermit's bed. The man closed his eyes and lay quietly. The emperor was worn out from a long day of climbing the mountain and digging the garden. Leaning against the doorway, he fell asleep.

When he rose, the sun had already risen over the mountain. For a moment he forgot where he was and what he had come here for. He looked over to the bed and saw the wounded man also looking around him in confusion. When he saw the emperor, he stared at him intently and then said in a faint whisper, 'Please forgive me.'

'But what have you done that I should forgive you?' the emperor asked.

'You do not know me, your majesty, but I know you. I was your sworn enemy, and I had vowed to take vengeance on you, for during the last war you killed my brother and seized my property. When I learnt that you were coming alone to the mountain to meet the hermit, I resolved to surprise you on your way back and kill you. But after waiting a long time there was still no sign of you, and so I left my ambush in order to seek you out. But instead of finding you, I came across your attendants, who recognised me, giving me this wound. Luckily, I escaped and ran here. If I hadn't met you I would surely be dead by now. I had intended to kill you, but instead you saved my life! I am ashamed and grateful beyond words. If I live, I vow to be your servant for the rest of my life, and I will bid my children and grandchildren to do the same. Please grant me your forgiveness.'

The emperor was overjoyed to see that he was so easily reconciled with a former enemy. He not only forgave the man but promised to return all the man's property and to send his own physician and servants to wait on the man until he was completely healed. After ordering his attendants to take the man home, the emperor returned to see the hermit. Before returning to the palace the emperor wanted to repeat his three questions one last time.

He found the hermit sowing seeds in the earth they had dug the day before. The hermit stood up and looked at the emperor.

'But your questions have already been answered.'

'How's that?' the emperor asked, puzzled.

'Yesterday, if you had not taken pity on my age and given me a hand with digging these beds, you would have been attacked by that man on your way home. Then you would have deeply regretted not staying with me. Therefore, the most important time was the time you were digging the beds, the most important person was myself, and the most important pursuit was to help me.'

'Later, when the wounded man ran up here, the most important time was the time you spent dressing his wound, for if you had not cared for him he would have died, and you would have lost the chance to be reconciled with him. Likewise, he was the most important person, and the most important pursuit was taking care of his wound.'

'Remember that there is only one important time and that is now. The present moment is the only time over which we have dominion. The most important

> person is always the person you are with, who is right before you, for who knows if you will have dealings with any other person in the future? The most important pursuit is making the person standing at your side happy, for that alone is the pursuit of life.'
>
> **The Emperor's Three Questions** by Leo Tolstoy

So, what have creativity and mindfulness got to do with this story? Well, mindfulness, as you know, is non-judgmental present moment awareness. In being fully in the moment like the hermit, totally absorbed in the activity of your choosing, you create an opening for your spirit to flow forth uninhibitedly, without getting chained by every negative feedback or critic.

Renew your intent for the week by repeating your declaration to the universe at the beginning of Part B.

Day 1

Exercise 1: Belief Balloon

TIME
15 to 20 minutes

STEPS
1. Think of a belief that is holding you down (specifically the belief about lacking talent). One way of doing this could be to list all your beliefs until you find one that hurts. For example, in my case, it used to be, I don't have what it takes to be a world-class author.
2. Repeat the 'Getting to Ness' exercise.

3. With your eyes closed, imagine a hot-air balloon being held down by four ropes. The balloon represents the belief holding you down and the behaviours that go with the belief. The ropes are the reasons you have the belief. They stand for evidence, emotion, logic and social feedback.

   In my case, the rope of evidence was, I have not published a major book yet. The rope of emotion was, I'll grudgingly live with my dream of becoming an author because it's better than trying and failing. The rope of logic was, look at how many books world-class authors sell; you've not sold any, while the rope of social feedback (though well-intentioned) was, 'You've achieved other things, so don't let this one thing bother you.'
   Intensely visualise your belief balloon straining at its tethers one more time.
4. Now, pick a new belief. In my case, it was, I can definitely write a bestseller.

   In your mind's eye, release the ropes of the balloon and replace them with thrusters. Thruster one is the new evidence to support your new belief. In my case it was, I've written stories for kids. That means I can write a bestseller too. Thruster two is the new emotion. In my case, it was, I feel immensely grateful to be able to impact so many people with my book on creativity through mindfulness. Thruster three of new logic was, the world today really needs this book, and the fourth thruster was, you have applied these principles of mindfulness in your own life. Now you must share them with others!

   Your turbocharged new belief balloon is now ready to take off!
5. Gently open your eyes with a smile and come into your environment. In your creativity journal, write down your new belief in big bold letters. Alongside, list five

specific things you will do (action) and say (words) that will make you live your new belief from this day on.

I started doing a number of things, like writing down ideas that seemed like good starting points for a book, reading relevant articles, fine-tuning ancient mindfulness practices into the ones you find in this book, trying them out, and teaching them to people who were learning mindfulness from me. I started telling people that I was writing a book I had long dreamt of, began to speak to designers and meditators as I connected the dots further, and said no to meetings that would interfere with my writing. And between you and me, I started practising Getting to Ness and then visualising myself as a bestselling author—bells and whistles included!

Completing this exercise took me 20 minutes and thrust me fully into the game! Is it worth your time? I think so. In fact, I continue to use it to manifest what I want into my life.

Day 2

Repeat the exercise from Day 1.

Day 3

Repeat the exercise from Day 1.

Day 4

Exercise 1: Getting to Ness

Exercise 2: Breathing Into The Heart

TIME
10 to 15 minutes

STEPS

Find a comfortable and upright place to sit. Take a few deep breaths, observing the flow of your breath as you inhale and exhale.

When you feel ready, gently bring your focus to your heart, and as you breathe in, feel your heart opening and softening. As you breathe out, release any tension or resistance.

Now bring an image of yourself into your heart or repeat your name and hold yourself in your heart, tenderly and gently. Silently repeat, 'May I be freed from self-doubt, may I be happy, may all things go well for me.'

Keep breathing into your heart, holding yourself with love and repeating the words. This will generate a deep, loving kindness and appreciation for yourself. Finally, whenever you are ready, take a deep breath and let it go. Then go about your day with a caring heart and a smile on your lips.

Day 5

Exercise 1: Self-compassion Meditation

TIME
10 to 15 minutes

STEPS

Begin this exercise by sitting in a position that is alert yet relaxed. Notice your posture and make any adjustments to it. Become aware of your breath as it moves in and out of the body. Just breathe normally, naturally and notice how it is. It could be short or long, tight or relaxed. Merely note it matter-of-factly. Continue to do this for two to three minutes.

When you feel ready, shift your awareness to your thoughts and emotions. Again, observe without judgement and matter-of-factly. Yes, this thought is one of planning, there is a feeling of impatience, there is a noise, yes, it is like this. Continue to do this for two to three minutes.

When you are ready, explore the question, 'What is difficult in my life right now?'

Whatever comes up—even if it's nothing—just hold on to it matter-of-factly. Yes, this too is there. In your mind's eye, look at it kindly and gently as you would look at an old friend; maybe even smile in kind acceptance. Continue to do this for two to three minutes.

Open yourself up to anything that is possible. Acknowledge and accept that we don't know how even the next moment or the next breath will be. Yes, it is like this. Continue to do this for a minute or so.

Take a deep breath and let your awareness rest gently on it as you continue to breathe normally thereafter. Continue to do this for a minute or so.

Whenever you are ready, gently open your eyes and return to your surroundings.

Exercise 2: Writing Meditation

TIME
10 minutes

As you have done many times already, you are writing just for yourself. You don't have to share anything you don't want to. In this exercise, you have 10 minutes to write free flowing about whatever comes to you. Just keep the pen moving and surprise yourself. For today, use the prompt, 'If I were my coach or advisor, I...'. Write what you would say to yourself about the opportunities and difficulties in your life right now.

Day 6

Repeat the exercises from Day 5.

Day 7

Exercise 1: Genie Check-in

In this practice, you will say hello to your creative genie and check in on how he is doing. Is he awakening, saying something to you maybe? Or does he need a little more time? Whatever comes up, don't judge it. Self-compassion works wonders with genies.

A few questions that might help your genie conversation:
    How many days did you practise?
    What was easy and what wasn't?
    Were there any other feelings or thoughts that surfaced?
Use your journal to record whatever comes up.

Over time, these check-ins will also provide a blueprint of your creative journey—one you can reflect on and share if you choose to help others on their journey.

Exercise 2: Mindful Meanderings

Choose a creative space in your town or city. It could be any place that epitomises creativity for you—a gallery, museum, music school or even a café or a park. Plan to spend a leisurely amount of time here, soaking up the atmosphere and getting inspired. Carry your journal to record anything that arises. This is your creative oxygen tank. Revisit the feelings evoked on this day whenever you need an extra dose of inspiration.

    As we tackle our beliefs—they can be hard nuts to crack—there is likely to be doubt, anxiety and demotivation. Failure and setbacks will come by to visit. In dealing with these lingering emotions, we need compassion towards oneself.

Dr Kristen Neff, a leading authority on self-compassion, says it has three components:

Mindfulness: Being aware of mental or emotional phenomena without getting attached to them or over-identifying with them and suffering averse reactions.
Common humanity: Recognising that failure and suffering are part of life and human experience and are not to be taken as 'something wrong with me'.
Self-kindness: Meeting oneself with warmth and kindness instead of ignoring aspects of oneself or being too self-critical.

Contrary to what it seems like, self-compassion is not easy. We may feel that if we accept ourselves as we are, we won't be motivated to change or improve. We may also feel that we'll become lazy, that in loving ourselves a little more, we could become unethical.

But research comes to the rescue again. A series of studies by University of California, Berkeley's Juliana Breines and Serena Chen shows that an attitude of acceptance is actually constructive. They evaluated how participants responded to setbacks, mistakes and their own weaknesses, and the evidence suggests that contrary to initial impressions, people with self-compassion are more likely to have a growth mindset, more likely to want to fix a past ethical transgression, and more motivated to improve and put in more effort improving. 'Self-compassion may increase self-improvement motivation given that it encourages people to confront their mistakes and weaknesses without either self-deprecation or defensive self-enhancement', they concluded.

The takeaway: Self-compassion is a good way to meet challenges.

17. WEEK 6: ACKNOWLEDGING OUR LIMITED KNOWLEDGE

Congratulations! You have made it to the final week of this magical journey!

You have met different enemies of creativity, understood them and in embracing them, have weakened or even destroyed them. With all the skills you have acquired, you are now ready to meet the trickiest of the anti-creativity brigade! Trickiest because this goblin is so clever that he often appears in our lives as a good friend and supporter of creativity. If you have ever come across a wolf in sheep's clothing, this is it.

Mr Cocky, with his know-it-all attitude is the last of the anti-creativity goblins we have to deal with.

> A Zen university professor had heard about a famous Zen Master and was intrigued that people spoke of him so highly. 'What could he know that I don't?' he wondered. One day, he decided to find out, so he went to visit the famous man. While the master quietly served tea, the professor, eager to display his knowledge, went on and on about Zen. He filled the visitor's cup to the brim, and kept pouring. The professor watched the overflowing cup until he could no longer restrain himself. 'It's full! No

> more will go in!' the professor blurted. 'This is you,' the master replied. 'How can I show you Zen unless you first empty your cup?'

On your journey thus far, you've delved into myriad aspects of creativity and mindfulness. Unlike the university professor in this story, you already know the importance of having a beginner's mind and listening deeply to what is told to you.

But it's always nice for us to get inspired, and the inspiration this time comes from a little bear called Winnie the Pooh.

Let's see how he connects with Mr Cocky.

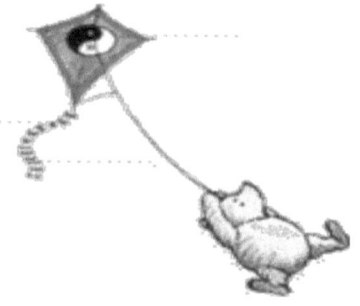

Winnie the Pooh has a certain way about him, a way of doing things that has made him the world's most beloved bear. Pooh's Way, as Benjamin Hoff brilliantly demonstrates in his book, *The Tao of Pooh*, is strangely close to the ancient Chinese principles of Taoism. Hoff's book explains Taoism through Winnie the Pooh, and talks about the bear through Taoism. You understand what AA Milne meant when he said he didn't write the Pooh books for children in the first place.

Over centuries, classic Tao teachings have been developed and divided into philosophical, monastic and folk religious forms. But basic Taoism is simply a way of appreciating, learning from, and working with whatever happens in everyday life. From the Taoist point of view, the natural result of this harmonious way of living is happiness.

One of the basic principles of Taoism is *Pu*, meaning uncarved block. In essence, it means that things in their original simplicity contain their own natural power that is easily spoilt or lost when that simplicity changes. This principle applies to people as well. Or bears. Which brings us to Pooh, the epitome of *Pu*.

When you discard arrogance, complexity, and other things that get in your way, you'll discover the mysterious secret known to Pooh: Life is fun. Along with this comes the ability to do things spontaneously and have them work, odd as that may appear to others. As Piglet put it, 'Pooh hasn't much brain, but he never comes to any harm. He does silly things and they turn out right.'

The other characters in the story are also wonderful embodiments of human qualities. While Owl's little routine is for knowledge for the sake of appearing wise, donkey Eeyore's is for knowledge for the sake of complaining, and Rabbit's is knowledge for being clever. The Eeyore attitude gets in the way of things like wisdom and happiness, and prevents any sort of real accomplishment. Cleverness, which Rabbit has in plenty, has its limitations—its mechanical judgements and clever remarks tend to prove inaccurate with passing time, because it doesn't look deeply into things to begin with. The thing that makes someone truly unique is something that a clever person cannot really understand.

Our own journey of creativity and mindfulness is best exemplified in this lovely conversation between Pooh and Piglet:

'Rabbit's clever,' said Pooh thoughtfully.

'Yes,' said Piglet, 'Rabbit's clever.'
'And he has brain.'
'Yes,' said Piglet, 'Rabbit has brain.'
There was a long silence.
'I suppose,' said Pooh, 'that's why he never understands anything.'

Renew your intent for the week by repeating your declaration to the universe at the beginning of Part B.

Day 1

Exercise 1: Mindful Listening

TIME
10 minutes

You will need a partner for this exercise. They should just be willing to speak to you for about five minutes after you complete the first step of this exercise.

STEPS
1. Repeat the breath awareness meditation for five minutes.
2. Your partner will speak uninterrupted for about five minutes. This will be a monologue. If they run out of things to say, that's fine. You can wait in silence until they have something to say again. You are not allowed to speak. Your job is to listen only. You are not even allowed to ask questions. At best, you may acknowledge that you are listening by nodding or saying 'hmmm' or 'I see'.
   Prompts for your partner could be, 'What is going on in your life?' or one thing they really want to do in life, or what challenges they are facing. They are also welcome to speak about anything they want. What is important

is that the topic should not be related to you. It could be about them or any other subject. The purpose of this exercise is to try and silence the inner voice of judgement that starts to speak as soon as someone speaks. The voice that says, 'I know better' or 'How stupid' or 'Hey... you know what, I have a similar story to tell. Only that mine is more interesting!' Along the way, the exercise may help some of us realise that Earth does not revolve around us.

It is also important to remember that you are not trying to impress anyone with your response, which you won't be asked for. You are listening completely immersed without mentally preparing a response at the same time; giving the speaker the full gift of your attention and experiencing what it is like to have a truly empty cup!

Exercise 2: Writing Meditation

TIME
10 to 15 minutes (or as long as you want)

As you have done many times already, you are writing just for yourself. You don't have to share anything you don't want to. In this exercise, you have 10 minutes to write free flowing about whatever comes up to you. Just keep the pen moving and surprise yourself. As prompts, use the following questions.

1. How did you feel when listening during the exercise?
2. Did you notice your mind wandering? If so, what was the distraction?
3. What helped to bring your attention back to the present?
4. Did your mind judge while listening? If so, how did it feel in the body?

5. Were there times where you felt empathy? If so, how did this feel in the body?
6. How did your body feel right after listening? What are you feeling right now?
7. What would happen if you practised mindful listening with each person you spoke to?
8. Do you think mindful listening would change the way you interact and relate to others?
9. How would it feel if you set the intention to pay attention with curiosity, kindness, and acceptance to everything you said and everything you listened to?

Day 2

Repeat the exercise from Day 1. Extend the skill of mindful listening to more conversations in an informal manner.

Day 3

Repeat the exercise from Day 1. Extend the skill of mindful listening to more conversations in an informal manner.

> *Be careful of your thoughts, for your thoughts become your words. Be careful of your words, for your words become your actions. Be careful of your actions, for your actions become your habits. Be careful of your habits, for your habits become your character. Be careful of your character, for your character becomes your destiny.*
>
> Chinese proverb, author unknown

Dwell on this ancient wisdom. What we think is often what we say and that, in turn, becomes input for the person who hears the words. Words move people. Words move nations and create history. Words are symbols of what is going on inside us, our heads and bodies. We share fear, joy, love, sorrow and dreams with our words.

Words lead to action, some we never think possible. So, watch the thoughts that create the words that create the actions. We can create or destroy. Over time, many actions become repetitive and even unconscious. Some are good and beneficial, others are not. Someone can be neat, clean, well-mannered; another, messy, dirty and rude.

Habits shape who we are. They become our character, our stamp of individuality. People know us by our character. They describe us as, 'He is a very creative guy' or 'She is a happy person'. Thoughts and actions build habits and character.

If our character is positive, others respond positively to us. If we are characterised by negative thoughts, judgements and gloom, others won't like to relate to us. Unless of course, they are similar (and that is even worse!). The way others relate to us defines a lot of what we think and say and act out, so there can either be a positive cycle that shapes our life or a negative cycle. Our destiny can be joyful, energising and uplifting. Sure, we might fail or fall in between, but if our habit is to get up, dust ourselves and move on with a smile, destiny smiles back. People then want to be around us. They want to know how we create all those wonderful things in our lives. They want to know where all the creativity and abundance comes from. And neuroscience is never too far away.

Psychiatrist Regina Pally says, 'According to neuroscience, even before events happen, the brain has already made a prediction about what is most likely to happen, and sets in motion the perception, behaviours, emotions, physiologic responses and interpersonal ways of relating that best fit with what is predicted. In a sense, we learn from the past what to predict for the future and then live the future we expect.'

Bit of a mind-bender, that? Not really. We are already telling ourselves and others the stories of our lives and how it is going to be, and then act in ways that make those stories come true. This is largely an unconscious process, but now that we are mindfulness ninjas, we are going to use the power of our consciousness to bring greater certainty and possibility to the process of shaping our creative journey. We will change the stories we tell, and our lives!

I know it works, for I have done it myself. Innumerable times. For example, I used to dream of riding a Harley-Davidson. I was then just about as tall as the motorcycle. But as I grew up, I continued to nurse the dream and live the stories as much as I could. My father's moped would often transform into a cruiser in my mind, and I also collected pictures of cruiser bikes (these were the pre-Internet days).

For my 18th birthday, my dear friend Sunnie gifted me a pocket book on motorcycles and I spent hours poring over it and in my mind, completing many impossible missions on the pictured beauties. When I joined college, my father got me a motorcycle that was slightly better than his moped. The innumerable bruises and broken bones that followed as I rode it like a racer on some days and cruiser on other days were no deterrent. Some friends laughed at the impossibility of my dreams, but I rode on. I had posters in my room and would tell people I would one day own a Harley. In the 1980s, there were probably two car manufacturers in India and four motorcycle makers. Most people had not even heard of a Harley, leave alone seen one. And the idea of an 18-year-old claiming that one day he would ride one, was to most people, a boast.

Twenty years later, around 2008, Harley-Davidson announced plans to sell its bikes in India. An agonising wait followed before they started accepting bookings and eventually in 2010, I became the proud owner of a Harley-Davidson, one of the first to be sold here. It has a special emblem etched on the engine that reads: First to Ride. India. 2010.

By the way, I still have the pocketbook of motorcycles Sunnie gave me. It's a bit worn, and dog eared now, but still perfect for a summer afternoon dream. And of course, I still ride my Harley.

In this way, I have repeatedly envisioned a number of things and experiences in great detail, which subsequently manifested in my life. Many were just ideas that seemed impossible. But now, with the power of writing meditation and mindfulness to boost, I often feel like Alice in Wonderland when she says, 'Why, sometimes I've believed as many as six impossible things before breakfast.'

The key insights we will work on are:

1. Thoughts are powerful sources of energy.
2. Thoughts become words (stories) and actions (lives).
3. We will think of what we want in our lives and then use the power of words, stories and actions to manifest them in reality.
4. We will share these thoughts and stories with others and allow the universe to conspire with them and make our dreams come true.

The important thing is not to let the dream remain just a dream. The secret lies in articulating the dream, making space for it to grow, staying humble yet determined, and not letting Mr Cocky sneak his tricks in. Share the dream with others, remain receptive to what they say, accept encouragement and criticism with equanimity and keep working to achieve the dream.

> You see things; and you say, 'Why?' But I dream things that never were; and I say, 'Why not?'
>
> George Bernard Shaw

Day 4

Exercise 1: Getting to Ness
Exercise 2: Envisioning My Life

TIME
10 to 15 minutes

This is not a free flow writing meditation exercise. If you find it more helpful to be slow and thoughtful, you may do so. Remember, the more you verbalise, the more tangible and real it will become. There is only one rule—find fulfilment while having fun.

In your creativity journal, write down what your life would be like in five years. Write as if it were already true. Don't let the thought of impossibility stop you. Envision, discover and then manifest the future you dream of. Before you start, consider the following prompts: Five years from now, who are you and what are you doing professionally and personally? How are you feeling in life, in relationships? What do people say about you and how do they treat you?

> Yesterday is but today's memory, tomorrow is today's dream.
>
> Khalil Gibran

Day 5

Exercise 1: Getting to Ness

Exercise 2: Envisioning My Life

TIME
10 to 15 minutes

Consider the life you envisioned for yourself on Day 4. Read it and connect deeply with it.

Now, write about what might get in the way of this life coming true. How will you respond to those challenges skillfully as you continue to manifest what you dreamt of?

Day 6

Exercise 1: Getting to Ness

Exercise 2: Envisioning My Life

TIME
10 to 15 minutes

Consider the life you envisioned for yourself on Days 4 and 5. Read it and connect deeply with it.

Now, write about all those who may help you make this life come true—who you can share the dream with, who will support you. At some point in your journey, it may not be a bad idea to share your dream with them. It's amazing how many people are eager to help.

There is only one thing that makes a dream impossible to achieve: The fear of failure.

Paulo Coelho

Day 7

Exercise 1: Genie Check-in

In this practice, you will say hello to your creative genie and check in on how he is doing. Is he awakening, saying something to you maybe? Or does he need a little more time? Whatever comes up, don't judge it. Self-compassion works wonders with genies.

A few questions that might help your genie conversation:
How many days did you practise?
What was easy and what wasn't?
Were there any other feelings or thoughts that surfaced? Use your journal to record whatever comes up.

Over time, these check-ins will also provide a blueprint of your creative journey—one you can reflect on and share if you choose to help others on their journey.

Exercise 2: Celebrate

Throw a party, invite people over, spend some quiet time with loved ones, or even better, do something altruistic—whatever feels appropriate for you. But do celebrate because you have accomplished something truly significant; you have completed the 48-day programme of manifesting your creative spirit! If you have followed the instructions carefully and truly given yourself to the process, you have set off powerful forces inside you and in the universe. Watch them unfold in your life.

Just remember two things: Stay confident in your new abilities, and stay humble.

And here's another secret—repeating this course or taking someone else through it step-by-step will only enhance your creativity.

EPILOGUE

Less than a few decades ago, if you said you went running, people would have asked, who is chasing you? But today, the fitness industry thrives on our need to be healthy, because we now understand how fitness results in good health.

Similarly, aided by neuroscience, mental health will become increasingly important in days to come. Just like we know that working out strengthens our muscles and stopping can lead to flab and an unhealthy state, we will understand that the brain is no different. A bad mental diet can lead to poor mental muscles. Mental gyms that include meditation and the exercises in this book will produce lasting mental health, creative abilities and an overall sense of well-being.

Technology already aids meditation and will possibly make greater inroads into offering the benefits of contemplative practices on a large scale. Digital delivery systems and apps are widely used. This book, however, uses a more traditional approach that has evolved from self-learning, practise, sharing and teaching in the old-fashioned non-digital way.

It is my hope that the reader also realises through these chapters a method of connecting with a much larger canvas that goes beyond creativity. One that includes clarity, calmness, kindness, compassion and equanimity. I have been extremely fortunate to have discovered many facets of life through these practices and then share them in these pages. I pray that for you, it is the same.

ABOUT THE AUTHOR

Gopi Krishnaswamy is a senior executive turned mindfulness meditation teacher who walked away from conventional corporate success into Zen, learning from many masters, including staying at Zen Master Thich Nhat Hanh's Plum Village Monastery, and eventually becoming a teacher.

Today, he works at the confluence of mindfulness, creativity, leadership and well-being. He has over 25 years of corporate and entrepreneurial experience with leading global companies and, in his last full-time role, was the Managing Director at IDEO, the iconic design company.

Gopi is also a teacher at the renowned Search Inside Yourself Leadership Institute and is one of the first in India to teach the extremely popular SIY programme that was born at Google. He lives in Bengaluru and travels to teach mindfulness, creativity and leadership across India and the world.

When not teaching or farming, Gopi can be found riding his Harley across the countryside!

www.ingramcontent.com/pod-product-compliance
Ingram Content Group UK Ltd.
Pitfield, Milton Keynes, MK11 3LW, UK
UKHW041950230426
12048UKWH00008B/259